RAILWAYS TO THE COAST

RAILWAYS TO THE COAST

Britain's seaside lines past and present

Michael H.C. Baker

PSL

Patrick Stephens Limited

Front endpaper A Paignton-bound HST curves around the edge of Torbay south of Torquay station on the last leg of its journey from Paddington on a sunny October afternoon in 1987.

Title spread 2-8-OT No 5239 approaching Kingswear with a train from Paignton in August 1982.

Rear endpaper No 34027 *Taw Valley* departing from Chester for Crewe with the 'North Wales Coast Express', August 1989.

First published in 1990

British Library Cataloguing in Publication Data
Baker, Michael, 1937–
    Railways to the coast: a tour of Britain's seaside lines.
    1. Great Britain. Railway services, history
    I. Title
    385' .0941

ISBN 1-85260-058-6

Patrick Stephens Limited is part of the Thorsons Publishing Group, Wellingborough, Northamptonshire NN8 2RQ, England.

Printed by William Collins Sons & Co. Ltd., Glasgow

Typeset by Burns & Smith Ltd, Derby

10 9 8 7 6 5 4 3 2 1

Patrick Stephens Limited, part of Thorsons, a division of the Collins Publishing Group, has published authoritative, quality books for enthusiasts for more than twenty years. During that time the company has established a reputation as one of the world's leading publishers of books on aviation, maritime, military, model-making, motor cycling, motoring, motor racing, railway and railway modelling subjects. Readers or authors with suggestions for books they would like to see published are invited to write to: The Editorial Director, Patrick Stephens Limited, Thorsons Publishing Group, Wellingborough, Northants, NN8 2RQ.

CONTENTS

ACKNOWLEDGEMENTS AND BIBLIOGRAPHY

Many libraries, particularly local studies sections, provided invaluable material for this book, only a fraction of which ended up being used simply because there wasn't room for more, These include the libraries of the Record Office, Kew, the National Railway Museum, York, and those at Bodmin, Dorchester, Wareham, Poole, Winchester (a uniquely comprehensive collection of railway books), Brighton, Hailsham, Basingstoke, Canterbury, Norwich, Caister, Dunoon, Glasgow, Lancaster and Blackpool.

Also consulted were various editions of *Railway Magazine*, *Railway World*, *Trains Illustrated*, *Great Western Echo*, the Journal of the Irish Railway Record Society, *Five Foot Three* and many other preservation society publications.

Books consulted include the following:
The Blackpool Story, written and published by Steve Palmer and Brian Turner (1976, ISBN 0-95001-133-9)
Cornish Riviera, S.P.B. Mais (GWR, 1934)
Railways of the Southern Region, Geoffrey Body (PSL, 1984 and 1989)
Reflections of the Furness Railway, C.R. Davey (Lakeland Heritage Books)
British Trams and Tramways, Peter Johnson (Ian Allan, 1985)
Regional History of the Railways of Great Britain, various volumes, including Vol 1 *The West Country* by David St John Thomas, Vol 2 *Southern England* by H.P. White, Vol 4 *North East England* by Ken Hoole, Vol 8 *South and West Yorkshire* by David Joy, and Vol 11 *North and Mid Wales* by Peter E. Baughan (David & Charles).
Pre-Grouping Atlas and Gazetteer, W. Philip Conolly (Ian Allan, 1965)
Harmsworth Atlas and Gazetteer (1909)

Left The Poole–Newcastle train, linking the south and north-east coasts, climbs away from the shore up Parkstone Bank in September 1989.

Left and below The author at Dungeness on the Romney, Hythe & Dymchurch Railway in August 1946, aged 9, in a picture taken by his father, and at the same spot a few years later in May 1989, photographed by his wife.

INTRODUCTION

The story of our railways and the resorts around our coast is one of high adventure, farce, tragedy, wheeling and dealing and also a good deal of ordinary, everyday comings and goings. There would have been no resorts on the scale that we know them had there been no railway system, and the hard times that both went through, and in some cases are still going through, are more than coincidental. In short, their fortunes are inextricably linked.

The railways were instrumental in virtually creating most of our seaside resorts. Brighton, the first, is an excellent example. Until the arrival of the railway it was the most fashionable place in Britain, with the Royal Pavilion at its heart, the seaside home of the monarch. But once the railway arrived, Queen Victoria lost interest, feeling that the place had been vulgarized by the advent of the masses, consequent upon the cheap and convenient travel the railways afforded, and she sold the Pavilion to Brighton Corporation in the late 1840s for £50,000 (compare that to the umpteen millions its present restoration is costing). In its place she and Albert created Osborne House, again beside the sea, on the Isle of Wight.

At the other end of the social scale were the masses. Barely tolerated by the management they would be grudgingly crammed into open four-wheeled carriages and trundled off to the seaside. But it was soon realized as vast crowds assembled at the main-line termini, that there was much profit in such business. Southend was a great attraction for Londoners, and the Blackwall Railway, later the London, Tilbury & Southend, set about capturing much of the traffic which had hitherto gone by water. Nevertheless, steamers continued to run from Tower Pier to Southend, Clacton, Margate and Ramsgate until the 1960s, only succumbing to railway electrification and, of course, road competition. There are some fascinating reminders of those early days in the museum at North Woolwich station.

Up on the Clyde Coast land/sea rivalry was equally fierce and there were a vast number of lines competing with each other and with the steamers. Again the steamer services survived into modern times, and could be said to have not wholly disappeared, for the last ocean-going paddle-steamer, the *Waverley*, was built by the LNER in 1947, and still does regular runs out of Glasgow down the Clyde, where she is based; she also covers the entire coast of Scotland, Wales and England each year, and indeed crosses the Irish Sea to Dublin.

The Dublin & Kingstown was the first railway in Ireland. Now electrified, it is one of the most scenic routes in the British Isles, running for much of its length beside the sea. Indeed I've been drenched more than once, alighting from a train, by winter storms breaking over some of the stations around Dublin Bay. Bray became the most popular resort in Ireland as a consequence of the railway and today special weekend and evening excursions, with commentaries, are run by the DART electrics.

Up in Belfast there was an equal demand for trains to take excursionists to the sea, and when the railway from Belfast to Larne was opened, Whithead, beside the shores of Belfast Lough and now the headquarters of the Railway Preservation Society of Ireland, came into existence as a resort and a pleasant place to which to retire.

The story of Blackpool and its excursion traffic would make a book in itself. If ever a resort owed its prosperity to the railway, this is it. Whole towns in the industrial north would shut their mills and the Lancashire & Yorkshire Railway would scour every siding to find sufficient carriages to take the workers in their tens of thousands to the sea. The town had three stations and miles of sidings, and well into the 1960s rakes of non-corridor carriages, still steam hauled, were a familiar sight on Saturdays and Bank Holidays around Preston heading for Blackpool from Manchester and many other towns and cities. Sadly, Blackpool Central, within a few yards of the

Tower, was so valuable a site that British Rail sold it off in the early 1970s and one of the other two surviving stations is threatened, though there is still a fair amount of traffic.

Southport and Morecambe are two other Lancashire resorts virtually created by the railway, and the lines to both were electrified before the First World War. New Brighton in all truth could never have been the most appealing of resorts, but its proximity to Birkenhead and Liverpool made it enormously popular at the turn of the century and it, too, was served by a pioneer electric line. Its once grand tower has long gone and with the fearful poverty and recession Merseyside people are suffering it is a ghost of a place today, although its electric trains still do good business. Across Liverpool Bay the North Wales resorts of Rhyl, Llandudno, Colwyn

The Severn Estuary seen from a Newcastle-bound HST north of Severn Tunnel Junction.

Bay and others owed much to the London & North Western Railway.

Meanwhile, on the East Coast, the North Eastern Railway built magnificent stations at Whitley Bay and Tynemouth, all wrought-iron and glass, to cater for the thousands of Geordies from the shipyards. The Whitley Bay and Tynemouth railway was another city to seaside line electrified in Edwardian times to cope with the enormous traffic it carried. Although it fell on hard times in the 1960s, its story has a happy ending for it now forms part of the splendid and tremendously busy Tyneside Metro, and Whitley Bay station has been sensitively restored.

In the prosperous south, although in the West Country some resorts have lost their branch lines, only Hayling Island and Selsey of the Hampshire, Sussex and Kent watering places have lost theirs, whilst the many others do such good business that all are now served by frequent electrified services.

There are many descriptions in Arnold Bennett's novels of excursions from the Potteries to North Wales resorts, as well as to the Isle of Man, though perhaps the finest of all is his description of Brighton, 'vaster than imagining of it. Edwin had only seen the pleasure cities of the poor and of the middling, such as Blackpool and Llandudno. He had not conceived what wealth would do when it organized itself for the purposes of distraction . . . Edwin could comprehend lolling by the sea in August, but in late October it seemed unnatural, fantastic.'

Edwin Clayhanger had arrived at Brighton by Pullman, a 'gilded vehicle'. The Brighton and South Eastern companies made great use of Pullmans to carry the superior classes between the capital and the sea. The Southern Railway introduced the all-electric 'Brighton Belle' in 1933 and such was its fame that all 15 of its carriages have been preserved. The very first electric line in England was Magnus

Volk's which opened at Brighton on 3 August 1883 and is still running, although the first in the British Isles was another seaside line, the Giant's Causeway in Northern Ireland, which beat Volk by a month. Not surprisingly, people were apprehensive of the new-fangled electricity, so to prove that it had been satisfactorily tamed the engineer removed his trousers in front of the Ministry of Transport inspectors and sat on the live rail!

The term 'Cornish Riviera' was coined by the Great Western Railway, and that company became prosperous and remained on a sounder financial basis than all others throughout the 1930s and '40s because of the tremendous holiday traffic it carried to the Dorset, Somerset, Devon and Cornish resorts. Two former GWR seaside branches which have closed, the West Somerset and the Kingswear, are now operated by steam preservationists, whilst a fascinating West Country revival has been the former LSWR Seaton branch. Narrow gauge electric trams now carry holidaymakers down to the sea, operated by a company which originated on the seafront at Eastbourne. Meanwhile, the main-line holiday business to the West Country resorts, along that famous stretch of railway beneath the red cliffs of Dawlish, is still so extensive that many trains only convey passengers who have reserved seats.

Whilst it is true that since the Second World War the motor car has carried the bulk of holidaymakers and excursionists to the seaside, a surprising number still go by train. For many people, a ride on a preserved steam train is part of their holiday by the sea, and with roads and car parks in resorts reaching saturation point, environmentalists and local authorities in places such as St Ives are looking at such schemes as 'park-and-ride'; the railway may well yet be seen as the saviour of many overcrowded resorts and their hinterlands.

THE WEST COUNTRY

Beginnings in the Far West

The image of Cornwall most often projected is that of a county devoted to the holiday industry, of picturesque fishing villages, golden beaches and richly wooded valleys, of a people chiefly engaged in the manufacture of Cornish pasties, seaside rock and garish paintings of golden sunsets, and enjoying the mildest climate in Great Britain. All this can certainly be found. It was the Great Western Railway which coined the term 'Cornish Riviera' and it has stuck; but it is misleading.

Until the last half-dozen or so generations, life for Cornishmen and women was a harsh struggle against nature, whether as fishermen, miners or farmers. Camborne and Redruth, in western Cornwall, were the centre of the tin and copper mining industries, and although these industries are now almost dead the scars they left and the sprawl of commercial and residential building they generated have resulted in a landscape quite without charm. Whilst eastern Cornwall is full of green valleys and fields, the windswept west end is much harsher.

As a result of this industrial development, Cornwall has as good a claim as any, although it isn't often recognized, to be the home of railways. Plateways had long been

Left The 12.40 Penzance–Paddington draws into Exeter St Davids on 31 March 1973.

used by the mines and the man who made the first successful steam locomotive was a Cornishman, Richard Trevithick. Born in Camborne on 13 April 1771, his father was a 'Captain' or manager of a mine and young Richard's first job was in a mine near his home looking after the engine. He was intelligent and much interested in improving the performance of the steam engine and to this end conducted various high-pressure experiments, building a number of models. His first full-size locomotive was designed to run on roadways rather than rails and he had it completed on Christmas Eve 1801. However, like many mechanical contrivances produced at Christmas it did not last long, although its demise was due more to the inability of the roads of the day to cope with a heavy machine and to certain minor problems rather than to any grave design faults. It ran away out of control, turned over and blew up. However, Trevithick continued his work and many coal mines in South Wales as well as Cornish tin, copper and clay mines purchased his engines — one of his high-pressure stationary pumping engines built in 1800 was still working 70 years later.

The world's first successful steam locomotive came about as the result of a wager between two Welsh mine owners. One bet the other that Trevithick couldn't build a locomotive which could travel a given distance pulling a load. On 13 February 1804 Trevithick's machine ran for $9\frac{3}{4}$ miles from Penydaren to Abercynon in South Wales pulling a load of ten tons of iron, handsomely

fulfilling the conditions of the wager.

Cornwall, and the lives of its people, was to be transformed by the railway. One associates Cornwall primarily with the Great Western Railway, but that company's first train did not enter the county until the opening of Brunel's Royal Albert Bridge on 2 May 1859. Prince Albert rode across the great bridge in the Royal Train, then walked back from Saltash station across it, examining the works with interest and understanding, for he was a great believer in scientific and technological progress. Later he was guest of honour at a banquet at Millbay station, Plymouth. Brunel, sadly, was unable to be present — he was abroad, attempting to recover from what proved to be his final illness, and although he did travel across his Royal Albert Bridge it

Above Former Pullman camping coaches beside Mounts Bay, August 1987.

TORQUAY

FREE BROCHURE FROM PUBLICITY OFFICER · MARINE SPA · TORQUAY

Left Torquay, seen on a GWR poster of the 1930s.

was as an invalid lying on a specially constructed couch, and he died early in the
autumn of that year.

The Great Western was essentially an
English company, despite its Cornish and
Welsh connections, but Cornwall did have a
number of railways of its own. The Poldice-
Portreath Tramroad opened in 1812, and
others followed, at least three pre-dating the
first public steam-operated railway, the Liverpool & Manchester. However, on all the
motive power was horses and the traffic exclusively mineral, copper in the case of the
Poldice to Portreath and the Redruth and
Chacewater lines, china clay on the Pentewan
Railway.

The Poldice-Portreath line is virtually
prehistoric in railway terms, was always worked by horses, never officially carried
passengers and had gone by the late 1860s,
but the other two survived into the steam era
and did convey a certain amount of passenger
traffic. No doubt there were occasions when
an employee or perhaps an adventurous small
boy or other local hopped aboard a Poldice-
Portreath wagon, but the first record of a trip
to the sea by rail in Cornwall would seem to
be on 30 January 1826 when three wagon-
loads of officials of the Redruth & Chacewater
Railway were wound down on the end of
rope from Wheal Buller to Narabo quays and

A 'Western' in charge of a Penzance to Paddington
express on the shores of the Teign Estuary, September
1976.

returned up the hill by horsepower.

The Redruth & Chacewater was of 4 feet
gauge, and steam appeared in 1854. Brakes-
men were employed, but no special vehicles
were provided for them and they had to
manage as best they could balancing
precariously on the wagons, as did miners
when travelling by train. Presumably if any of
them had the temerity to point out to the
management the risks they were running on
the company's behalf, the reply would be that
these were a good deal less than the miners
faced below ground. Chacewater was never
reached — not the first, or last line to prom-
ise more in its title than it ever achieved.
Prosperity depended entirely upon the state of
the mines and as these gradually closed so the
line faltered. Nevertheless, it reached its century, the last train running on 25 September
1915.

The Pentewan was a narrow gauge line of
2 ft 6 ins. Although primarily dependent
upon the china clay trade, it did carry passengers, both regular ones and excursionists,
from St Austell down to the harbour, and
thus the seaside, at Pentewan. Horses and
steam locomotives worked together on dif-

ferent sections of the line for some time, but at the end, in March 1918, two steam engines had a monopoly. The superior facilities of the harbours at Par and Fowey were chiefly responsible for the line's demise.

These three lines were purely Cornish, and local at that, important enough to the community they served, but not what one thinks of as a proper, complete railway, carrying both goods and passengers, and linked to the national system. By virtue of its geographical position at the south-western extremity of Great Britain, the natural flow for any traffic through Cornwall, other than the purely local, was from east to west or vice versa. Traditionally the traffic had gone by sea, but two railway companies came into existence in 1846 to take it over and to construct the main line linking the port of Penzance with the county town of Truro, and thence on across the many river valleys, including the greatest

of them all, the Tamar, to Plymouth.

The West Cornwall Railway grew — inevitably — out of a mineral line. This was the Hayle Railway which had opened between Hayle and Redruth, with branches, in 1838.

It was different from, and superior to, the other Cornish mineral lines in that most of it was steam operated from the start. It was also of 4 ft 8½ ins gauge. Carriages were provided, the passenger service being inaugurated on 22 May 1843.

It was the intention of the West Cornwall

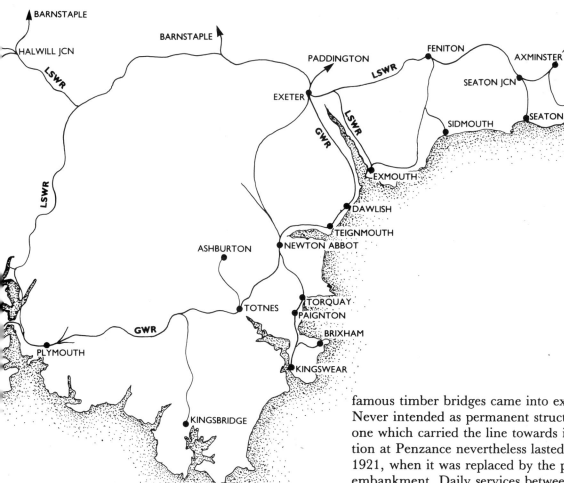

to reconstruct the Hayle line to broad gauge and use it as part of a through route from Penzance to Truro where it would connect with the Cornwall Railway, and to this end it was temporarily closed in 1852 for the rebuilding and regauging to take place. Brunel was engineer of both the Cornish main lines but as it happened he had to supervise what was initially a standard gauge line for the money could not be found for regauging. Financial restraints also dictated that the viaducts should be of wood, so Brunel's

famous timber bridges came into existence. Never intended as permanent structures, the one which carried the line towards its destination at Penzance nevertheless lasted until 1921, when it was replaced by the present embankment. Daily services between Penzance and Redruth began on 11 March 1852, to a temporary station above Truro in August of that year, then to one beside the River Fal in 1855, and finally to the present Truro station in 1859.

Falmouth, although older than many resorts, is not an ancient port, having come into existence in the seventeenth century. By 1688 it was the mail station for the West Indies, but some 150 years later it lost the contract to Southampton, chiefly because the Hampshire port was linked by railway to London. The Cornwall Railway came into existence to attempt to regain the port's importance and construction began in 1846. The enthusiasm shown by the citizens of Falmouth was not shared by other Cornishmen, some of whom rioted against the navvies when they began to work on the line near Truro. It was not until 1863 that the $12\frac{3}{4}$ miles between Falmouth and Truro was completed, eight viaducts being required in order to cross the valleys it encountered. As elsewhere in Cornwall their spans were of timber, and the final example was not replaced until 1934.

Meanwhile, by May 1859 the Cornwall Railway had its broad gauge line from Plymouth to Truro ready. This, too, had taken a long time to build, nearly 12 years, but no Cornish company ever found it easy to raise capital, and in addition there were many valleys to cross, necessitating no fewer than 34 viaducts in the 54 miles. Again Brunel employed timber for the spans.

With the joint leasing of the West Cornwall Railway by the South Devon, the Bristol & Exeter and the Great Western railways in 1865, it was possible to finance the addition of broad gauge to the existing standard gauge tracks, and through passenger trains began to run between Paddington and Penzance on 1 March 1867. The transformation of the county was about to begin.

Until this time, practically all goods going beyond the county borders were taken by sea, but the opening of the through line to Plymouth and beyond killed coastal trading almost instantly, resulting in the decline of many of the ports, for which fishing could not compensate, whilst the era of the holiday visitor had hardly begun.

The main line from Saltash to Penzance extends for 76 miles and on it there is scarcely a straight piece of track. It tends towards the south rather than the north coast, although there are only two points where one can actually see the English Channel. These are at Par, beyond the station where the line curves around the harbour, and the final, splendid section, $324\frac{1}{2}$ miles from Paddington, where the train bursts under a bridge east of the site of Marazion station to follow the great curve of the bay for all but two miles into Penzance station.

Clay and surf

The most westerly of the Cornish seaside branches, that to St Ives, $4\frac{3}{4}$ miles long, can claim all sorts of distinctions. Scenically it is distinguished, historically it was the last section of new broad gauge mileage, whilst in modern times it is frequently cited as the prototype for the 'park-and-ride' solution to those seaside resorts beset with a summer excess of motor cars and a dearth of suitable parking places but fortunate enough to have kept their railway line. Lelant Saltings station, just under a mile from where the branch leaves the main line at St Erth, was opened in 1978 specifically for visitors to park their cars and then ride in comfort to St Ives.

S.P.B. Mais in his book *Cornish Riviera*, published by the Great Western Railway in 1928, says of St Ives: 'It is doubtful whether there is a more popular seaside resort in England'. Painters in Victorian times were entranced, not only by the scenery, but also particularly by the especial quality of light, and flocked there. They have continued down to the present time; although it has to be said that for every piece of art of any quality produced in the village there are many hundreds which can charitably be described as less than mediocre.

The St Ives branch was opened by the West Cornwall Railway in June 1877 and carried both goods and passengers right from the start. Through carriages used to run to and from London, being detached at St Erth. At one time, on summer Saturdays in the 1950s, the 'Cornish Riviera Express', no less, used to complete its journey there rather than at Penzance. Since the end of steam and the termination of goods services, St Ives station has been reduced to a single track and platform served solely by a diesel multiple unit or railcar, so no signalling is necessary beyond St Erth.

Some 25 miles up the coast is Newquay. In its railway heyday it was served by two lines; they approached it from opposite directions and minerals and a canal featured in their origins. Our interest begins in June 1876

A St Ives train formed of a Collett 'B' set hauled by 2–6–2T No 4566 leaving Lelant on 14 April 1960. (*Peter Treloar*)

when a passenger service began from Fowey, on the south coast, by way of Par, where connections were made with the main line, and then on north-westwards across the Luxulyan Valley by way of the 216 yards long, 98 feet high Treffry Viaduct, to Newquay. Within little more than a year the GWR had taken over the working from the owners, the Cornwall Minerals Railway, and on 1 July 1896 it absorbed the company.

Newquay's other line was the last branch to be built in Cornwall. It ran from a triangular junction with the main line at Chacewater and reached Newquay by utilizing an existing mineral line from Shepherds, west of Perranporth. Appearing as late as 1905, and thus the creation of the GWR, it owed its origin more to passenger than goods or mineral demands, although the latter were still important.

S.P.B. Mais remarked: 'The great majority of people who stay in Newquay stay there because they know it to be the most convenient of all Cornish seaside resorts from which to explore the whole county.' Certainly Newquay itself is not to be recommended for its elegant architecture or olde worlde charm. Basically a late nineteenth century development, the only man-made artefact of much distinction is the ironwork on the Victoria Hotel. There is also a Great Western Hotel, dating from the early years of this century and once railway owned, whilst the pleasant, standard-pattern GWR station building beside platform 1 is now disused, being replaced by a box shoe-horned up against an estate agents which proudly sports a plastic frontage as ugly as it is long.

But few of us go to the seaside for aesthetic reasons and if you want superb, beautifully clean sandy beaches, the finest surfing in Britain and exhilarating bathing, then Newquay is the place.

The Chacewater to Newquay branch closed in February 1963 but the Par route survived, at $20\frac{3}{4}$ miles, and with five intermediate stations, the longest of the Cornish branches,

Above Newquay station in the 1880s. (*Author's collection*)

Below Newquay station in the 1980s.

stretching from the south to the north coasts. It passes through the heart of china clay country with miniature, white-topped Mount Fujiyamas of spoil and the chimneys of old engine houses, not all of them yet abandoned, dotting the horizon. There are also several ungated crossings, where the train slows to 5 mph; beside one, the Summer Lodge touring centre is a herald of the approaching seaside. It must surely have Second World War origins, for a number of its buildings have a very military look about them which a colourful paint scheme may disguise but not remove.

Despite much of Newquay yard having been given over to a Co-Op store, the station still possessed in 1988 three platforms and some sidings. All of these are needed on summer Saturdays, for the Newquay branch is the only Cornish one still regularly served by long-distance expresses.

Fowey, like Newquay, was once served by two branches. That from Lostwithiel began as a broad gauge clay line in 1869, was closed, converted to 4 ft 8½ ins and reopened in 1885, when passenger services began. Known as the Lostwithiel & Fowey Railway, it passed to the Fowey's other line, the Cornwall Minerals Railway, in 1892 and thence to the Great Western. It is easy to overwork the description 'picturesque' when describing Cornish coastal towns and villages, but what else can one call Fowey? On the south coast, some seven miles west of Looe, the little port has a ferocious past, a bloodthirsty catalogue of raids by and retaliations on various foreign powers. Pirating and smuggling were first nature to Fowey folk. Life had become rather less rumbustious, and perhaps duller, by Victorian times when the railway arrived to liven things up again.

Two passenger routes to a small seaside town with limited accommodation was a bit of luxury, and the line from Par became goods only as long ago as July 1929. Dr Beeching proposed ending passenger services on the Lostwithiel route alongside the Fowey River and this came about on 4 January 1965. Previous generations might have given the

same treatment to the demon doctor as they gave to King Edward IV's messenger — they cut off his ears — but the 1960s Fowey citizens were rather more refined and merely expressed regret at their loss. The Par route was converted to a lorry-way, but the Lostwithiel line remains and is the busiest goods branch in Cornwall, carrying vast quantities of china clay down to the English China Clay wharves at Fowey Docks.

Unlike the other minerals mined in Cornwall, china clay is of fairly recent origin. Its suitability for porcelain was discovered around 1746, and by 1900 most was being exported, through Charlestown (near St Austell), Par and Fowey. It reached the ports by various methods, horse and wagon, narrow and standard gauge railway, and pipeline. The latter proved much the most efficient, and gradually the purely industrial lines closed, although the famous Plymouth and Dartmoor line continued in use until 1960. None the less, railways were still needed to transport clay from the pipelines, and regular trainloads continue to run to Stoke-on-Trent for porcelain making, but much more is exported from Par and, above all, from Fowey.

Should we take note of the Helston branch? It did not, after all, reach the seaside, but it *was* intended to reach the Lizard, the most southerly point on the mainland of Great Britain. It opened from Gwinear Road on the main line to Helston in May 1887 and was always worked by the GWR. Plans for putting Helston on the railway map had been afoot for over 40 years, so naturally the citizens of the home of the Cornish floral dance were overjoyed and the usual banquet and fireworks display were indulged in when the great day finally arrived and goods and passengers trains began work.

The GWR actively pursued the notion of a light railway on to the Lizard, and at the turn of the century this was estimated as costing £85,000. But Helston was about to ensure its footnote in the history books. On 13 August 1903 the Chairman of the Great Western Railway remarked: 'We have great doubts whether Light Railways so desired would be

Looe station, August 1987.

justified . . . We have also been considering
the cases in which independent persons run
motor car services along the roads to our
Railway Stations. We do not see why we
should not feed our own Railway ourselves by
means of motor cars . . . the first car will be
run shortly from Helston to the Lizard.' Four
days later, on Monday 17 August 1903, two
Milnes Daimlers 22-seater buses performed
the inaugural runs with due pomp and without mishap and thus inaugurated GWR bus

The 15.00 to Liskeard heads away from Looe, 30 August
1983.

services, an event which would have wide
scale repercussions on branch lines in Cornwall and throughout the GWR system.

The Looe branch began in 1860 as part of
a mineral railway, occupying the bed of what
began its career as the Liskeard and Looe
Union Canal. This ran from Moorswater,
which lay in a deep valley immediately north
of Liskeard and passed under the Plymouth to
Penzance railway on its way to the coast. For
several decades the independently owned
branch had no connection with the main line,
and when one was put in in 1909 the result
was one of the most precipitous stretches of
railway in the county. A separate station for
the branch was built at Liskeard, at right
angles to the main line so that branch trains

set off due north. They then swung round to the east, curved under the main line and continued until they had encompassed practically 360 degrees and had passed under the main line for a second time. At Coombe Halt, virtually under the main line viaduct, the branch train reversed and headed through the deeply wooded valley along the gradually widening river until it arrived at its destination.

Passenger trains still run to Looe and freight trains serve Moorswater, although the mineral lines north of here were closed at the time of the First World War and the wooden viaduct was long ago replaced by a graceful stone one. The railway helped Looe, picturesque and popular, to grow rapidly, for it was now little more than an hour from Plymouth. Indeed, in the 1930s the GWR had plans to bring it even nearer by building a direct line from St Germans, but this did not materialize.

The GWR took over the working of the Looe branch in 1909 but one of the Liskeard & Looe Railway 2-4-0Ts, *Lady Margaret*, dating from 1902, survived into the first year of nationalisation, although she had given way to Swindon-built tank engines on the line of her origin decades earlier.

In the summer of 1987 I travelled down to Looe in one of the four-wheeled railbuses which British Rail had just introduced and the squeaks and squeals as it curved down through the woods between Liskeard and Coombe would have set a pair of wooden false teeth on edge. To no one's surprise, older, bogie railcars rapidly re-appeared.

South Western rivalry

The Bodmin & Wadebridge is a most historic line. It was the first standard gauge line in Cornwall, it was the first to employ locomotives, and it never came into the Great Western empire. It did not actually reach the sea, but we are certainly entitled to consider it for it came into existence chiefly to carry sea sand, and many years, decades in fact, later it formed part of a route to the sea over which the remarkable 'Atlantic Coast Express' would run.

The railway opened on 4 July 1834 and passengers were carried free to mark the occasion. Its one and only locomotive was called *Camel*, built by the Neath Abbey Iron Company. All 12½ tons of it, along with tender, cost £725, then a second engine was delivered in 1836 and named *Elephant*. Both were sold in the mid-1860s, being replaced by two infinitely more up-to-date machines belonging to the London & South Western Railway, *Ajax* and *Atlas*, dating from 1840, and the handiwork of Messrs Jones and Potts. Eventually, in the last years of the last century, three of Beattie's celebrated well tanks were drafted to Wadebridge, chiefly for the Wenford Bridge mineral line, although they regularly worked further afield and often turned up at Padstow. By 1917 they were the last survivors of their class, but were still only middle-aged and were to last until the 1960s.

Inevitably much of the Bodmin & Wadebridge's traffic was minerals of one sort and another, for the district was sparsely populated. However, in 1840 an excursion was run from Wadebridge and other stations to see a public hanging at Bodmin. Unfortunately for Bodmin its railway was of no importance nationally. Its great rival had long been Truro and when the latter achieved main-line status decades before Bodmin and became the junction for the important Falmouth and Penzance lines, the battle was over. The new diocese of Cornwall, established in 1876, built its cathedral at Truro and the County Council, created 12 years later, set up its headquarters there.

The GWR, as we have seen, owned no railway mileage in Cornwall until 1866; nevertheless, it had from the outset regarded the county as being within its empire. The LSWR had other ideas. This railway had begun life as the London & Southampton in 1838 but had soon widened its horizons. Its moves westwards to Salisbury and Dorchester were intended as preludes to an assault on the heart of Great Western territory: Devon and Cornwall, and in a devilishly cunning move it acquired the Bodmin & Wadebridge Railway in 1846. The cleverness of this was not immediately obvious, for the nearest piece of LSWR track at the time was 200 miles to the east. Bodmin got itself connected to the rest of the British railway system in May 1887, though not as yet directly to the LSWR, for it was the Great Western who built a 3½ mile long single track branch from its main line at Bodmin Road to its own station at Bodmin General.

On 1 June 1895 the rest of the LSWR finally joined up with the Bodmin & Wadebridge when the North Cornwall line from Okehampton and Launceston was completed and through carriages, the forerunners of the 'Atlantic Coast Express', 'provided with lavatory accommodation and fitted with electric light', were put on to and from Waterloo. To quote the August 1900 *Railway Magazine*: 'When the old residents of this part of Cornwall look on these modern vehicles and contrast them with those in which they travelled to and from the market in their childhood days, they must realise to the full the great strides science and money combined have made in connection with our railways.' The fastest service, the 1 pm out of Waterloo, took 6¾ hours to Bodmin, and a third-class tourist return ticket cost 36s 6d (£1.82½p).

At Halwill Junction, some 13 miles from Okehampton, a line headed off westwards towards the little resort of Bude. It got as far as Holsworthy but took nearly 20 years to reach its destination, which it did in August 1898. Bude is relatively modern, unlike most Cornish seaside towns, although it is certainly a good deal older than the railway. Tennyson stayed here and, like generations since, marvelled at the waves and the surf.

A superbly produced little book entitled *Devon and Cornish Days* by E.P. Leigh-Bennett which the Southern Railway brought out in the early 1930s puts to shame anything that even the great and wonderful GWR publicity department brought forth. Leigh-Bennett says this of Bude: 'You can have anything you want here except the Pier-and-Bandstand type of holiday'. He goes on to praise the 'ex-

tremely good ''diggings'' ', and a hotel with 'bedroom window balconies on which you can sit on hot summer nights (when not doubling two hearts downstairs) and listen to the distant Atlantic song' and the 'delicious sound of the tractor moving along a fairway, than which I know of no more pleasant awakening in any place'. The station at Bude was of similar design to that at Padstow, a single platform, but was not so conveniently placed, being a good half-mile from the town.

It was not until 27 March 1899 that the most westerly point of the Waterloo empire was established when the line along the Camel estuary from Wadebridge to the port of Padstow came into use. One of the stations, Camelford, was advertised as the alighting point for Tintagel, and over the years the LSWR, the Southern and British Railways have made great play of its Arthurian connections. This culminated in the naming of the Southern Railway's first express engines after the Knights of the Round Table (No 777 *Sir Lamiel* has been preserved in the National Collection), but the class was too heavy for any member ever to visit the North Cornwall lines. Another locomotive, Brighton 'Atlantic' No 2425, was named *Trevose Head*, a headland which is within easy walking distance of Padstow, but once again the engine was unsuitable for the branch.

Eventually the problem was solved when the 'West Country' Class was introduced, and amongst the first members were Nos 21C106 *Bude*, 21C107 *Wadebridge* and 21C108 *Padstow*. Later came *Bodmin*, *Holsworthy* and others, all of which were able to, and did, visit the north Cornwall places from which they received their names. *Bodmin*, in its rebuilt British Railways guise as No 34016, was rescued by the Mid-Hants Railway from Barry scrapyard and has done much work on that line since 1979, being renamed by the Mayor of Bodmin in September that year.

Considerable ceremony accompanied the opening of the Padstow branch, the special train from Exeter conveying the LSWR General Manager who arrived to a rendition of 'See the Conquering Hero Comes' by

The westbound 'Devon Belle', hauled by No 35015 *Rotterdam Lloyd*, speeds through Clapham Junction on 20 July 1951. (*Brian Morrison*)

Padstow Artillery and Delabole Brass Bands. Leigh-Bennett has this to say of Padstow: 'Somehow a seaside terminus always multiplies one's pleasures by two. Added to which this is a very little terminus, with heaped fish boxes between the metals and a couple of trawler funnels peeping inquisitively over the edge of the quay alongside the platform.'

The railway approached Padstow by way of a quite impressive viaduct over the Little Petherick Creek. Above the station the LSWR erected the biggest hotel in the town, the Metropole, a not particularly beautiful pile of stone, concrete and grey pebble-dash. The date '1900' is boldly embossed on its façade.

Padstow grew, but not very much; the holidaymakers came, but not in enormous numbers. Plans existed for a light railway

along the coast to Newquay, and the GWR, noting this with disfavour, obtained powers to shorten its own principal line to Newquay with a cut-off from Bodmin Road; but nothing came of either scheme. Perhaps the most dramatic change the railway brought was in fishing. Fish could be sent directly and quickly to London, and by 1914 on a busy day up to 200 tons of fish would be dispatched in some 50 wagons. An ice works was set up, which also supplied electricity to the harbour, the station and the Metropole Hotel. During the First World War lock gates were fitted to make the inner harbour independent of tides and coaling berths were provided for steam drifters, whilst in Southern Railway days a big fish terminal was erected alongside the passenger station and the huge fishing fleets from Grimsby, Lowestoft and other North Sea ports called regularly. Padstow's heyday was shortlived, however, for in the 1930s fishing declined nationwide and the local boat-building industry also began to fall away. However, the holidaymakers still arrived in goodly numbers on summer Saturdays.

The Cornish Riviera

S.P.B. Mais, in his book *Cornish Riviera*, claims that 'it is because its climate . . . is the most equable in the world we claim the right to describe the Duchy as the Cornish Riviera'. The title Riviera would seem to be one conjured up for publicity purposes by the Great Western some 25 years before Mais was writing, in that astonishing first decade of the twentieth century when the company, awakening from the dormant years at the end of the broad gauge era, made such advances on so many fronts that by 1910 the other railway companies of the British Isles could only look on with a mixture of envy and admiration. The London & North Western might still call itself the 'Premier Line', but at the end of the Edwardian era it sounded a pretty hollow boast.

The Great Western's original route to Devon and Cornwall, going as it did via Bristol, was longer than the London & South Western's, 194 miles to Exeter against 171. By 1897 the beautiful Dean bogie singles were running the 'Cornishman' from Paddington to Exeter, the longest non-stop working in the world, in 223 minutes at an average speed of 51 mph, but in the 1900 timetables Dugald Drummond's excellent 4–4–0s enabled the London & South Western to reach Exeter ten minutes earlier. Something would have to be done!

The Great Western had long before got itself saddled with a contract with the caterers at Swindon station which insisted that every train stop there, notwithstanding the pretty poor fare it offered. However, as soon as the contract ran out in 1895 trains began to run through without stopping. The first was the 'Cornishman', the 10.15 am out of Paddington, and the company's crack express until the advent of the 'Cornish Riviera', its first stop now being Bristol Temple Meads. The Great Western had introduced the first corridor train in the world in 1892 and a year later the 'Cornishman' had a brand new set of Dean's corridor coaches allocated to it.

The introduction of the through corridor train was a great step forward. Ladies of nervous disposition might now relax, knowing that they could move away from unwelcome attention, that help could be easily summoned, and that the mere fact of the existence of

The 'Cornish Riviera', hauled by No 6008 *King James II*, accelerates past Old Oak Common at the start of its journey to the West on 22 March 1958.

through communication would deter many would-be molesters from attempting to pursue their evil ways. Lavatories were now accessible to all, and tickets could be much more easily checked. The advent of corridor trains also brought about the widespread introduction of restaurant cars and practically the first on the GWR was included in the 'Cornishman' in the summer of 1896. The company was now doing all it could to encourage the ever-increasing and more adventurous middle and lower ranks of the middle class to take its seaside holidays in the west. These might not yet be so affluent that they could venture abroad, as did the really well-off, but then was not the climate of Cornwall just as good as that of the south of France and northern Italy, without its extremes of heat — the English Riviera in fact?

So the Cornish Riviera came into being.

In 1904 *The Railway Magazine*, with the co-operation of the go-ahead General Manager of the GWR, James (later Sir James) Inglis, ran a competition for the title of a new train which the company was to introduce in July to the west, running non-stop between Paddington and Plymouth North Road, 246 miles in 265 minutes. Altogether 1,286 entries were received, and curiously, although 'Cornish Riviera Limited' was one of them, Inglis chose the more simple 'Riviera Express'. However, the new train very soon came to be known as 'The Cornish Riviera', sometimes with the suffix 'Limited', sometimes 'Express'. The first up train was hauled out of Penzance on 1 July 1904 by 'Bulldog' Class 4-4-0 No 3450 *Swansea*. Five of its carriages were Dean clerestory corridors, but the shape of things to come was seen in the sixth, the diner, which was a massive elliptical-roofed vehicle 70 feet long and 9 ft 6 in wide, designed by Dean's successor, George Jackson Churchward.

The following year the clerestories were banished, replaced by a complete rake of new Churchward carriages, the largest yet built for any British railway, and of such dimensions that they were banned from operating, not just off the Great Western, but even on some of its own more restricted lines. Not for nothing were they nicknamed 'Dreadnought' after the revolutionary battleship just introduced by the Royal Navy and swiftly copied for the Kaiser's High Seas Fleet.

The GWR's West of England record-breaker, No 3440 *City of Truro*, at Didcot in May 1989.

The GWR now had the most up-to-date trains in Britain, hauled by the most up-to-date locomotives, for Dean's singles had given way, first to Dean-influenced outside-framed 4-4-0s, and then to the pure Churchward — with American overtones — 'Atlantics' and 4-6-0s, the latter to set the pattern of locomotive development in Britain down to the end of steam.

But the GWR still had the longest route to the west. The next step was the building of a brand new main line which would give the GWR the shortest route to Exeter and thus finally vanquish the London & South Western. Parts of it already existed. There was the meandering Berks & Hants which linked Reading and Devizes by way of a single track, there was the Weymouth main line between Westbury and Castle Cary, and the final section of the Yeovil to Durston branch, Durston being the last station on the original main line before Taunton. By linking these up, and easing out, although by no means getting rid of, the sinuous curves, the 'Cornishman' could reach Exeter in 1906 in an even three hours at an average speed of 57.8 mph and the LSWR was beaten. Nearly 30 years later, in March 1933, as part of the Government's unemployment relief programme, further short, but important, cut-offs were constructed which enabled the 'Cornish Riviera', the 'Torbay Express' and other Paddington to West of England trains to avoid Westbury and Frome and reduce the journey time to the Devon and Cornish resorts still further.

In 1935 to mark its centenary the GWR bestowed upon the 'Cornish Riviera' a magnificent set of carriages, the prototypes of which were the eight 'Super Saloons' of 1931. Two years earlier the Pullman Car Company had signed a contract for its vehicles to work on the Ocean Liner boat trains between Plymouth docks and Paddington and shortly afterwards further vehicles went to work on the Great Western to form the 'Torbay Pullman'. However, for some reason Pullmans did not find much favour on the routes out of Paddington; the 'Torbay

Pullman' was withdrawn, the Pullman contract came to an end in December 1930, and to take the place of the Pullmans on the Ocean Liner specials — which moved over to the Southern Railway boat trains between Waterloo and Southampton and lasted into the 1960s — Swindon built eight carriages which were designed to outdo Pullman standards. No expense was spared and they made their first run in November 1931, conveying passengers from the maiden voyage of French Line's *Colombie*. The Centenary carriages were almost identical in appearance to Pullman cars with bulging sides to give the maximum space, and recessed doors. Although the interiors of the 'Cornish Riviera' trains were inevitably less luxurious than those of the Super Saloons they were still fine vehicles, quite the equal of Gresley's spendid 'Silver Jubilee' set, with which they were contemporary.

As with all the specially built luxury trains of the 1930s, the Centenary sets were broken up and put into ordinary service at the outbreak of war in 1939, never to be re-formed. When the 'Cornish Riviera' returned after the war it was formed of the latest standard stock, but still 'King'-hauled east of Plymouth, 'Castle'-hauled west of there, as it had been since 1927. In early BR days rakes of new Hawksworth flat-sided carriages were provided and these lasted, in red and cream livery, until the chocolate and cream BR standards took over. 'Warship' diesels replaced the 'Kings' in 1958, then came the magnificent 'Westerns', and today those superb HSTs work the train.

In the late 1960s and early '70s someone in high authority at British Rail headquarters took violently against the notion of named trains, around the same time that it was decreed that virtually everything BR owned should be the same shade of blue. The only named train officially left on the Western Region was the 'Cornish Riviera' and one only knew this from looking in the timetable — there was nothing on the train itself to proclaim its ancient title. Nowadays the publicity value of the old names and the goodwill they

engender is appreciated and the 'Torbay Express', the 'Cornishman', the 'Royal Duchy' and the 'Devonian', along with the 'Cornish Riviera', all once again run to and from the resorts of the West country. The 'Golden Hind' now has the once trendy 'Executive' tag attached to it and is a Pullman train, whilst two new titles are the 'Cornish Scot' and the 'Night Riviera'.

In 1987, the down 'Cornish Riviera', faster than ever, left Paddington at 10.50, stopped for one minute at Exeter St Davids, left at 12.46, got to Plymouth at 13.45, and then, stopping at the principal Cornish stations, arrived at Penzance at 15.42. The speed and power of the HSTs is equally effective whether on the high-speed stretches along the Thames Valley and through the Vale of Pewsey, roaring up the South Devon banks, or accelerating from the numerous Cornish stops and speed restrictions. The GWR toyed, perhaps not very seriously, with the notion of electrifying the Devon and Cornwall main line, but that was more than 50 years ago and it would seem certain that the 'Cornish Riviera' will go into the next century diesel-powered, perhaps still with the HSTs.

Brunel and South Devon

The line Brunel built for the South Devon Railway from Exeter on to Teignmouth and Newton Abbot is, quite simply, the most famous piece of seaside railway in the land. It is certain that our present-day concern for the environment would prevent anyone building a railway line beneath the cliffs of a particularly fine stretch of coastline, but things were different in Victorian times; if one had the cash and could claim it was in the sacred cause of scientific or technological progress, then one could get away with almost anything. Now, having been there for over 140 years, the railway line is such an accepted part of the land and seascape, the object of generations of small boys' waves, postcard manufacturers, holidaymakers, and enthusiasts' camera lenses

and tourist departments' panegyrics, that if anyone should ever propose its removal there would certainly be a concerted roar of protest!

Had the system of propulsion Brunel intended for the line west of Exeter succeeded then surely the career of the steam locomotive on the railways of Britain and the rest of the world would have been a short one. The steam railway was scarcely 20 years old in the mid-1840s and it was by no means certain that other forms of propulsion might not yet prove superior. The most promising rival appeared to be the atmospheric system. It had first been used on another seaside line, along the southern stores of Dublin Bay from Kingstown to Dalkey in 1843. After two visits to the Dalkey line, Brunel recommended that the atmospheric system should be used in South Devon. Had it proved reliable it would certainly have become universal. Just imagine the advantage of this swift, quiet and clean mode of propulsion over the smoke-belching, clanking steam locomotive.

But the system did not prove reliable. The technology of the time could not match the brilliance of the idea. It proved very difficult to cast the pipes to a sufficiently small tolerance, level crossings and points created great complications, the stationary steam engines were required to work at extremely high pressures, and, worst of all, the vacuum could not be maintained. The line opened from Exeter to Teignmouth in May 1846 and to Newton Abbot in December of that year, steam operated by locomotives borrowed from the GWR, and it was not until January 1848 that the atmospheric trains began a regular service. Speeds of up to 64 mph were averaged with trains of 28 tons, and 35 mph with a 100-ton load, the latter certainly comparable to steam propulsion.

The greatest advantage of the atmospheric system was expected to be in hill-climbing, and thus gradients over the difficult stretch of line around the southern slopes of Dartmoor between Newton Abbot and Plymouth were deliberately made severe, so that construction costs could be kept down. But atmospheric trains never worked west of Newton Abbot and ever since then the operating department has had to contend with the restrictions the switchback nature of the line has imposed on speeds and loads.

Throughout 1848 the problems grew, breakdowns and delays became commonplace and in June of that year Brunel called it a day. It was a brave decision for this great engineer to take, for his directors urged him to continue, but he knew that the problems were insuperable. The other atmospheric systems fared no better, the Irish line going over to steam in 1855.

The South Devon Railway thus had to build itself a fleet of steam locomotives, all tank engines, such being considered more suitable for the severe gradients and the fairly short distances characteristic of the South Devon Railway. In 1866 the 'Associated Companies', as the Great Western, the Bristol & Exeter and the South Devon were known, took over the Cornish main lines, and from that date the South Devon provided the motive power for all trains west of Exeter until the time came for it to be absorbed by the GWR, on 1 February 1876.

Once clear of the city of Exeter, swinging along an elevated route over the Exe, past the suburban station of St Thomas, recently beautifully restored by Sainsbury's and partly incorporated into their adjacent superstore built on former dockland, the views which make this stretch of railway unique begin. The Exe widens and becomes big enough to accommodate coastal motor ships, and Powderham Castle (after which one of the first 'Castle' Class engines, No 4080, was named) can be seen on the up side of the track, but is often missed for all eyes tend to be on the down side.

Now the train is running along the water's edge. Speed drops, as a 65 mph restriction applies around the coast and the line curves first one way then another, swinging through Starcross where one can look down through the planks of the wooden platform to the water beneath and where the famous pumping house built for the Atmospheric Railway has been restored as a museum to the ill-fated but fascinating project. At the end of Star-

A Class '45' accelerates away from Dawlish Warren with a Paignton to Newcastle express in August 1981.

cross pier a ferry runs over to Exmouth which, if one is travelling in the up direction, can by this nautical means be reached a good deal quicker than by staying on the DMU bound for the same destination which has to make nine stops up one side of the Exe and back down the other.

The line passes over various creeks and streams before Dawlish Warren, where a number of camping coaches, used by railwaymen, are stationed. These are painted in GWR chocolate and cream, although the last genuine Great Western camping coaches disappeared fairly recently, being replaced by BR Mark 1s and, rather curiously, two LMS-designed former inspection saloons. The line now curves sharply westwards until it is running beneath the famous dark red cliffs, and we are on the most celebrated section of this celebrated railway. Dawlish station, still with its Great Western Railway cast-iron nameboard on its often seaswept up platform, overlooks both promenade and town. Running beside cast-iron railings, curving underneath a cast-iron footbridge, our train now plunges right through an outcrop of the cliffs and will do so several times more before

Teignmouth station, with its elaborately detailed and painted cast-iron awning supports, is reached. Some expresses stop at both Dawlish and Teignmouth, which are small resorts — Teignmouth also has a harbour — but most passengers will have their eyes on Torquay and Paignton beyond the Teign estuary.

Here we leave the sea, for the time being. The train turns inland along the east bank of the Teign estuary which narrows as Newton Abbot comes into view. The station is large and impressive, although somewhat less so since the big signal boxes and the many gantries of semaphores disappeared in the spring of 1987. The sea is still no great distance off, Torquay being six miles away, Paignton eight. For Plymouth and Cornwall-bound trains the fierce climbs begin at Aller Junction, but Torbay trains head for the palm trees and sand.

A Class '47' at the head of a Newquay to Paddington express runs along the sea-wall at Dawlish on a wet summer Saturday in early September 1987.

Torbay

From its inception the South Devon Railway had wanted to build a line to the growing resort of Torquay, but at first it obtained parliamentary permission to go only to Torre and no further. As any viewer familiar with *Fawlty Towers* (and who isn't?) will be aware, Torquay has always considered itself distinctly up market, and such aspirations do not always permit too close a contact with the railway.

During the Napoleonic wars the aristocracy was prevented from taking its pleasures abroad and thus turned to English resorts. Brighton was the first but Torquay soon followed, for its situation was highly pictur-esque reminiscent of the French and Italian rivieras, and the climate was mild and kind to invalids. The town grew rapidly, and villas reminiscent of those to be found on the shores of the Mediterannean and the Italian lakes sprang up on the wooded slopes. When the railway arrived the population was already in excess of 11,000 and there were some 2,000 hotel bedrooms — the railway could certainly not claim to have created Torquay. But it did add further to its popularity. An independent line, the Dartmouth and Torquay, was formed, and in August 1859 passenger trains began to run through from Torre to a station in Torquay proper and thence to Paignton.

Torquay has a handsome station, dating from 1876. It is built of stone and brick in the French chateau style, liberally hung with flowering baskets, its platforms planted with palm trees. However, it has only two plat-forms, which is hardly generous for so grand a resort, and in steam days there were times when it was quite inadequate. In 1957, for in-stance, on the peak Saturdays between 22 June and 14 September, 94,464 long-distance passengers arrived. The greatest number on any one of those days was 16,433 on 10 August. If we reckon that a ten-coach train carried 640 passengers, then this meant at least 25–26 trains. This takes no account of the heavy local traffic which had to be fitted in amongst the long-distance trains.

Newton Abbot provided the motive power for many of the Torquay line trains, and anything from a 'King' to an 0–6–0 might be expected to turn up. With the line's severe speed restrictions and gradients, the smaller-wheeled classes could handle the lengthy but slow-moving trains nearly as successfully as the four-cylinder express engines. For a period in the late 1950s and early '60s, the big Churchward '4700' Class 2–8–0s regularly worked the 'Torbay Express' to and from Paddington.

Paignton has always been a bit down market compared to Torquay, although it probably has the better sands. The line on from Torre, skirting the sea in several places, was not an easy one to build, the steep initial descent incorporating a series of bridges, a tunnel (later opened up) and a viaduct.

The 'Torbay Express' title was bestowed on the long-established 12 noon out of Padding-ton in the early 1920s. The summer 1932 timetable notes that it is a 'Luncheon and Tea Car Train'; it reached Exeter at 2.53 pm, left there six minutes later and got to Torquay at 3.35 pm. Its final destination was Dartmouth which it attained at 4.18 pm, a remarkable feat since it ran out of railway at Kingswear. Dartmouth, then as now, was reached by ferry (although there is no indica-tion of this in the timetable!) for the land-owners on the western side of the River Dart had refused to let the railway cross the river beyond Greenway Tunnel and come into Dartmouth, as the Dartmouth & Torbay Railway, which had built the extension down to Kingswear in 1864, had planned and hoped. Not that the trip across the river isn't a pleasant conclusion to the journey from Paddington; it is indeed, and most fitting as from Exeter onwards the sea is such a dominating presence.

The immense popularity of its holiday ser-vices to Torbay persuaded the Great Western Railway to use some of the money which the Government provided to help relieve unemployment in the early 1930s to double the track from Paignton to the next station, Goodrington Sands, put in extensive extra

Above A Class '25' climbing towards Torre with a Paignton to Plymouth train in September 1976.

Below A Paignton-bound HST curves around the edge of Torbay south of Torquay station on the last leg of its journey from Paddington on a sunny October afternoon in 1987.

Above The 'Torbay Limited' at Paddington on 21 August 1926. (*Author's collection*)

Below No 7827 *Lydham Manor* running rounds its train at Kingswear on 1 September 1983.

carriage sidings between these two points, and to improve the line on to Kingswear so that the largest locomotives, the 'Kings', could use it. All this was done in 1931.

There is one station between Goodrington Sands and Kingswear, at Churston, and from here a branch two miles long was built to the fishing port of Brixham, home of the famous trawlers. In later years this was worked by an auto-train in charge of an 0-4-2T, and one of the regulars, No 1466, is now preserved by the Great Western Society at Didcot.

When holiday traffic resumed at the end of the Second World War it rapidly increased to proportions never previously experienced, which was highly gratifying as far as receipts were concerned. However, track occupation on Friday nights and Saturdays in summer reached saturation point and the Western Region introduced a scheme whereby all passengers to the West of England had to book a seat at the same time as they bought a ticket. Although the late 1940s and '50s, before a car for each family was the norm, was the high point of holiday rail travel, it is worth noting that such is still the demand on the Western Region in summer that the scheme is still in force.

By 1972 British Rail decided that there was no profit in running services beyond Paignton, being heavily used during the relatively brief summer season but not much

2-8-0T No 5239 approaching Kingswear with a train from Paignton in August 1982.

at other times. The Dart Valley Light Railway had been successfully operating steam trains on the nearby branch from Totnes to Buckfastleigh for three years and decided that it could do the same between Paignton and Kingswear. Using a mixture of paid and voluntary workers, it commenced services in late 1972 as soon as BR gave them up.

The Brixham branch was closed and taken up by British Rail but the steam operation of the Kingswear line has proved a great success. Seven-coach trains packed with holidaymakers and trippers depart every half-hour during the peak summer period for a 6¾ mile journey on one of the most picturesque stretches of railway in the British Isles.

Devon and the LSWR

The resorts of south-east Devon were exclusively the preserve of the LSWR. They were, and are, not very large and all were served by single-track branch lines. Such lines

fared badly in the Beeching years and all but one has disappeared, although another has experienced a unique reincarnation.

Exmouth is the second largest town in East Devon and has been a port for over 700 years. When Exeter's maritime status began to decline in the early nineteenth century, a new dock was built at Exmouth in the hope that the trade could still be kept on the River Exe, but it was not very large and the river was too shallow for it to have much effect. Nevertheless coasters still regularly call there.

The South Devon Railway had advertised Starcross station, across the estuary, as 'Starcross for Exmouth', ever since its opening, and the ferry still operates to this day. Even though since the Exmouth line became part of the Western Region some through trains have operated around the coast from Dawlish, up the west side of the estuary to Exeter and then down the east side to Exmouth, it is still much quicker to abandon the train at Starcross and complete the journey by boat. However, for passengers from Exeter and beyond the opening of a direct line to Exmouth in May 1861 was of considerable advantage. The Exmouth line leaves the main line $1\frac{1}{4}$ miles east of Exeter Central at Exmouth Junction and runs for $9\frac{1}{4}$ miles along the banks of the Exe. It might have been laid to the broad gauge for there was a plan to link it with the South Devon, but in the event the LSWR worked it from the outset, although it was independently owned for the first five years of its existence.

Five miles along the coast from Exmouth is the resoundingly named Budleigh Salterton, reached by the railway in 1897 by means of an extension from Tipton St Johns on the Sidmouth branch. Sidmouth, seven miles to the north-east and rather larger than Budleigh Salterton with a good many hotels and Regency-style villas, had been connected with the main line since July 1874. A line $8\frac{1}{4}$ miles long ran from the village of Feniton, although the station built there was called Sidmouth Junction, with intermediate stops at Ottery St Mary and Tipton St Johns. Six years after the Budleigh Salterton to Tipton St Johns line was opened, the LSWR extended it westwards to link up with Exmouth, this coming into use on 1 June 1903.

Moving east again we come to Seaton, at the end of a branch opened in March 1868. Four miles long, it ran from what had originally been known as Colyton station on the main line. This was later renamed Seaton Junction, as a more convenient station in Colyton proper could now be opened on the branch. The railway prompted Seaton's growth into a resort of modest proportions, although its bathing facilities were limited, its dangerously sloping beach being mainly shingle.

Left One of the short-lived railbuses at Exmouth in the summer of 1987. Across the estuary is the former GWR West of England main line.

Right The terminus of the Seaton tramway, May 1988.

One final East Devon line deserves our attention, although it served a resort which was just across the border into Dorset. This was the Lyme Regis branch. It left the main line at Axminster, the next station to Seaton Junction, headed south to Combpyne, the only intermediate station, then turned eastwards and crossed the county border into Dorset on the outskirts of Lyme. It was unique amongst the seaside branches from the LSWR's West of England main line in that it made a connection in the London rather than the Exeter direction, so that in theory a train could run straight through from Salisbury and beyond without stopping, although there were precious few occasions when one did.

The Lyme Regis branch was a late arrival, not being opened until August 1903. The resort it served is the most famous, and probably the most picturesque, of any between Weymouth and Exeter. It will forever be associated with Jane Austen who wrote about the fashionable set from Bath who made it popular in the late eighteenth century, but its history goes back much further than this. Today it is a delightful place, somewhat reminiscent of a Cornish town, although dreadfully difficult to negotiate by road for its streets are narrow, steep and winding, and at holiday times parking is very difficult. It was a pity that it was not served by a main line for if it had its station would surely still do good

business; but this could hardly have been, for although the LSWR's West of England line comes within five miles, a deviation through Lyme Regis would have entailed much tunnelling and ferocious gradients.

Of the five south-east Devon branches, the only one surviving today is that to Exmouth. For a while it was served by the four-wheel Class '142' 'Skipper' railcars, some of which worked through to Barnstaple, Newton Abbot and Paignton, but they were soon banished from the West Country having proved themselves unable to negotiate sharp bends satisfactorily. They were replaced by elderly first generation railcars culled from all over the BR network. Exmouth station, which once boasted two island platforms, a goods yard, and an engine shed which was home to four steam locomotives, has been completely rebuilt and now consists of just one platform. Although so much reduced, the rebuilding has been sensitively done and Exmouth enjoys a good service; in the 1987 summer timetable there were 29 down trains and 27 up, with around half those numbers on Sundays. The six intermediate stations remain open and most trains call at all of them. Although the trains carry a fair number of holidaymakers and day trippers most of their revenue is made from commuters and shoppers.

The closures in south-east Devon all came in the 1960s and were not totally unexpected.

Like so many seaside branches, particularly those serving the smaller resorts, goods traffic never amounted to much: the passenger side was very busy from the middle of July to early September but for the rest of the year it centred around a small number of regulars and some casual business, which is not to say that the lines were not a valued asset to the community, their passing a matter of regret.

LSWR-built 'M7' 0-4-4Ts had long been familiar motive power on the Seaton, Sidmouth, Budleigh Salterton and Exmouth lines, while before them the 'T1s' and '02s', their Adams-designed predecessors of the same wheel arrangement, held sway. The Lyme Regis branch, however, was different. It was built as a light railway, to save costs, and thus suffered from severe weight restrictions and sharp curves. After various types had been tried out, the Adams 4-4-2Ts were found to be the most suitable and from 1916 they established a virtual monopoly. In 1957 a GWR '14XX' 0-4-2T was tried out but retired defeated as had so many types before. The end for the 4-4-2Ts eventually came in 1961 when the LMS Ivatt-designed 2-6-2Ts, which had proved so popular on many former SR and GWR branches, took over. Not that these lasted very long, being replaced by diesel multiple units $2\frac{1}{2}$ years later. These saw out the last days of the branch, closure coming in November 1965.

Perhaps rather unexpectedly, push-pull trains did not find favour on any of the lines, except the Seaton branch. The Lyme Regis 4-4-2Ts were never push-pull fitted and the other lines were worked in conjunction with the Exmouth one, which carried too heavy a traffic for such operations, being in effect Exeter's one suburban service. Trains of up to seven carriages were common during the rush hour. Early in this century rail motors were tried out, in an effort to compete against the newly introduced Corporation electric trams, but they were unreliable and the 0-4-4Ts with rakes of non-corridor coaches remained the norm into the 1960s. British Railways-designed stock appeared in 1956, replacing many of the LSWR vehicles which went for scrap, although some remained, and there were Maunsell and Bulleid corridors for the through London services. This use of BR designed non-corridor carriages was almost unique on the Southern Region. 2-6-2Ts began to replace the 'M7s' from 1952, the year BR Standard Class '3s' of this wheel arrangement were first allocated to Exmouth Junction, but the process was gradual and some of the 0-4-4Ts lasted until 1960.

In 1970 a remarkable reincarnation began at Seaton. A 2 ft gauge tramway which had been operating beside the sea at Eastbourne had to find a new home and the trackbed of the former Seaton branch was chosen. The gauge was widened out to 2 ft 9 in and services began in August 1970. A variety of cars, both double and single deck, work the line; clerestory single decker No 14 incorporates parts of a London Metropolitan Electric car dating from 1906. A ride on the line is great fun and it now extends inland from Seaton along the Axe valley for three miles to Colyton.

THE SOUTH COAST

Dorset

Having tiptoed across the Devon border into Dorset by way of Lyme Regis, we now come to the first all-Dorset branch. The East Devon branches all being part of the London & South Western empire, it might be thought that the rivalry with the Great Western took place only west of Exeter. Not so. Few seaside towns were fought over more fiercely than Weymouth, and it was from the GWR's main line over which it ran its Channel Island expresses to and from Paddington that the Bridport line diverged at the village of Maiden Newton, $7\frac{3}{4}$ miles north-west of Dorchester.

It opened in November 1857, and although locally owned it was operated from the start by the GWR; like so many similar arrangements, the line was eventually bought by the GWR in July 1901. Few branch lines did not at some point have ambitions beyond serving their immediate locality or were not part of some grand scheme designed to thwart a rival. Thus it was that Bridport might have been served by the Devon & Dorset Railway, a GWR project designed to link Dorchester

A view of West Bay, Bridport, in the 1930s with a GWR clerestory camping coach in the station yard. (*Author's collection*)

and Exeter by way of Maiden Newton, Honiton and Sidmouth. The LSWR immediately retaliated with a proposed extension of its Southampton to Dorchester line which would have followed much the same route to Exeter. The latter received the approval of Parliament but the LSWR did nothing about it, beyond building their Dorchester station as though it had been part of the Exeter through route, thus causing all sorts of operating problems which were not finally overcome until the 1970s.

Running 9¼ miles through some particularly delightful and sparsely populated countryside, the Bridport branch had two intermediate stations, Toller and Powerstock, names which might well have been conjured up by Thomas Hardy. Despite its name, Bridport is not quite on the sea, being two miles inland, nor is it any longer a port. But it is a handsome town, famous for its ropeworks, and Bridport ropes were sent all over the world. They began their sea voyages at West Bay, two miles distant on the mouth of the River Brit — a small port but nevertheless thought worth linking with the railway, and this extension opened in March 1884.

The West Bay line did little enough business, goods or passenger, although Sunday school parties and the like made use of it from time to time. The last regular passenger train departed on 22 September 1930. Bridport itself, however, continued to make good use of its branch. There were nine trains in each direction on weekdays at this time and excursion fares were available from Dorchester, Weymouth, Bath and Bristol; at one time it was even possible to book an excursion from Paddington.

In the mid-1950s, pannier tanks worked nearly all the traffic, goods and passenger, but by the time I made my first journey on the branch in 1972 goods traffic had ceased and a single unit diesel railcar handled all the passenger traffic, making eight return journeys each weekday, none on Sundays. Stations, apart from Maiden Newton, were unstaffed. As the guard and driver gloomily commented whilst we sat chatting at Bridport station, 'They're determined to shut the line'. It closed in May 1975. There was no great furore, but it was a sad loss for those who relied on the railcar and its friendly crew, and those for whom the twisty, narrow country lanes precluded any chance of a substitute bus, which is never an adequate replacement for the train but can be better than nothing.

We all have our favourite resorts and mine is very nearly Weymouth. I had my very first seaside holiday there, at the age of one and a bit. We went by train, Southern Railway

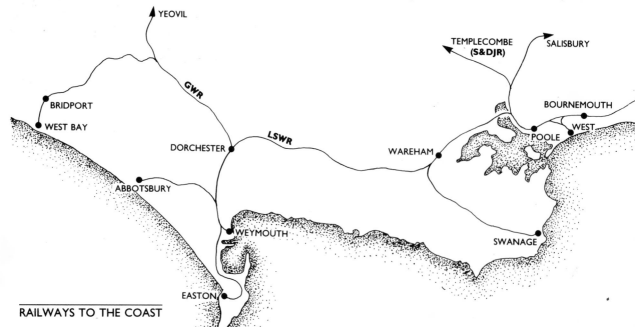

RAILWAYS TO THE COAST

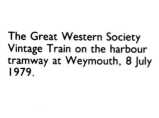

The Great Western Society Vintage Train on the harbour tramway at Weymouth, 8 July 1979.

from Waterloo. Weymouth has just about everything necessary for a really good seaside holiday. It is a busy, though not very large, port, with ancient, narrow streets leading down to the quayside. There is lots of attrac- tive if seldom spectacular architecture, there are magnificent sands, a bay of such beauty that Constable produced one of his finest paintings of it on his honeymoon, and a harbour tramway over which the Channel Island boat trains trundle — or rather used to — in and out of the Datsuns, Transits and Cavaliers.

The GWR and the LSWR arrived at Weymouth at the same time, 20 January

1857. The eight-mile line from Dorchester was the property of the GWR but the LSWR had running powers and consequently it was of mixed gauge. In 1865 the rails were extended down the quay to serve the Channel Islands steamers, operated by both the LSWR and the GWR.

Beyond Weymouth, jutting far out into the English Channel, is the great lump of rock known as the Isle of Portland. It is not a true island, being joined to the rest of Dorset by a narrow causeway, and along this a railway line was laid at the same time as the Weymouth harbour tramway. A great naval base had been built here during the time of the Napoleonic wars and it was extended and made ever more formidable throughout the last century. Enormous numbers of sailors were carried on the Portland branch, the GWR and the LSWR taking it in turns to work it. At first the branch extended only as far as the end of the causeway, but eventually another 3½ miles was blasted through the rock to the other side of the island at Easton, this section opening in September 1902.

Weymouth, with its station in the heart of the town and the proverbial stone's throw from the beach, attracted great numbers of both day-trippers and holidaymakers; large hotels were erected beside the Georgian terraces on the promenade, while smaller ones and streets of boarding houses sprang up beside the station, and the ancient port became a popular resort.

By the 1930s, however, Weymouth station had seen better days. Brunel's overall roof was demolished before the Second World War and there were plans to totally rebuild it but the outbreak of war postponed this. Although holiday traffic fell away, and the Channel Islands were occupied by the Germans,

Weymouth was very busy with military and naval specials, particularly in the build-up to D Day when a large section of the invasion fleet sailed from Weymouth and Portland.

Weymouth shed was the property of the GWR, and although there was also a very small LSWR depot, that company's nearest proper shed was at Dorchester. In later days Western engines at Weymouth moved over to make room for Southern ones and by 1967 the Great Western had vanished, leaving the all-conquering Bulleid 'Pacifics' and some BR Standards in sole occupation. The 'Merchant Navy' Class, by this date the most powerful steam express engines in ordinary service on British Rail, ended its days at Weymouth, and the shed closed when steam finished on the Southern Region on 9 July 1967. A housing estate was built on the site and virtually all that remains of the shed which lasted for 110 years is a street called Great Western Terrace.

The once busy Portland line had closed in March 1965. A certain amount of naval traffic still came by train but the number of ships and the crews belonging to them had declined enormously from the Edwardian heyday of coal-fired Dreadnoughts, and it was simpler and cheaper to provide road transport from Weymouth station.

With nationalization Weymouth became part of the Southern Region. The writing was finally on the wall for this bit of Brunel's empire, and at the beginning of the 1960 season Channel Islands boat trains were transferred

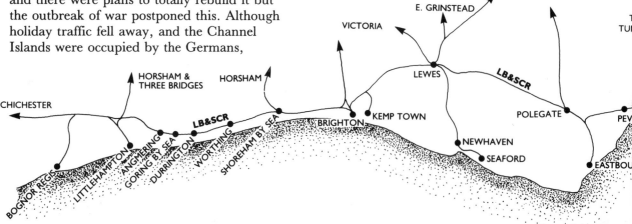

from Paddington to Waterloo. The GWR-built main line between Dorchester and Castle Cary was singled and apart from trains for South Wales and specials, all long-distance holiday services were eventually banished from it and sent by way of Basingstoke, Southampton and Bournemouth.

The long-promised rebuilding of Weymouth station finally got under way in the mid-1980s and a new, smaller, but attractively designed building was opened in the summer of 1986. The number of platform faces was reduced from the one-time maximum of eight to three, the handsome goods

shed, after serving for a while as a garage, was demolished, the carriage sidings were considerably reduced in number and a funfair and superstore moved in on the site. The new station is still just as conveniently sited very nearly beside the sea and across the road from the bus and coach terminus, and, perhaps best of all, electrification of the main line between Bournemouth and Weymouth was completed early in 1988. With this came 24 spendid new trains, the Class '442' Wessex Electrics. They are such an advance in comfort and riding qualities over their predecessors, the 4REPs, that it is a wonder how those old horrors were tolerated for so long. Although the '442s' are passed to run

THE SOUTH COAST

along the Weymouth harbour tramway, propelled by a diesel locomotive, none has yet done so. This meant that in 1988 for the first time since it was opened, no boat train used the line and its future looks bleak.

A seaside branch which had a very quiet existence and disappeared in the early days of nationalisation was the six-mile long line from Upwey Junction, on the main line from Dorchester to Weymouth, to Abbotsbury. There was one intermediate station, at Portesham, and although there had been hopes when the branch opened in November 1885 that local quarries might yield stone and iron ore traffic, this did not materialize and the line had to rely on passengers. These seldom warranted more than the regular one-coach autotrain, and the line closed in November 1952.

Wareham, 22 miles from Weymouth, used to be where one changed for the Swanage branch. Although this closed in 1972, the preservationists, latterly with the enthusiast support of Network SouthEast, are ensuring that before long we will be able to do so again. The branch, which leaves the main line at Worgret Junction, a mile west of Wareham, is still operated by BR as far as Furzebrook to serve clay works and the largest on-shore oil field in the British Isles. From Swanage, $3\frac{1}{2}$ miles back as far as Harmans Cross, the branch has been relaid and is operated as a preserved steam railway by the Swanage Railway, one of the most popular tourist attractions in Dorset with the enthusiastic backing of both the County Council and local people. At Corfe Castle is one of the most picturesquely situated stations in the country which, beautifully restored by its tenant, Les Hayward, now awaits the trains,

The Swanage Railway is probably the biggest tourist attraction in Purbeck. This Tony Kerins poster for the 1990 season depicts LMS '2MT' No 46443 leaving Swanage, with the paddle-steamer *Waverley* rounding Old Harry out in the bay.

A Weymouth-bound 'Wessex electric' passing the Pullmans of the Venice-Simplon Orient Express, Bournemouth, July 1988.

Above One of the magnificent new Class '442' Wessex Electrics heads across Poole Harbour with the 'Royal Wessex' from Weymouth to Waterloo at dawn on a spring morning in 1988.

Below A holiday home in a farmyard at Stoborough, close to Poole Harbour. The carriage is thought to be the former SER royal saloon of 1851.

which will continue on from there to link up with BR at Furzebrook; the running of steam trains over BR's part of the branch seems to be only a matter of time.

Between Wareham and Parkstone there are a number of locations where the railway runs beside and even across Poole Harbour, said to be the second largest natural harbour in the world. Traffic has steadily increased over the years and since electrification the number of trains between Bournemouth and Wareham has doubled. Poole station, which is very near the water, was given a most inadequate rebuild in the 1960s, but this was put right when a far larger and infinitely more handsome building was completed in 1988. The first Poole station, opened in 1860, was on the opposite side of the Quay at Hamworthy, and although passenger traffic ceased long ago it is still used for freight from the docks.

Controversy surrounds the future of Bournemouth station. Situated inconveniently far from the town centre, on account of the toffee-nosed attitude of certain citizens in the nineteenth century who wanted all the benefits of a railway without any of its disadvantages and therefore insisted it be kept well out of sight, rebuilding is urgently needed. It is listed and therefore cannot be knocked down, but its draughty inhospitality really should be replaced by a handsome, well-equipped, comfortable, modern building forming part of a bus, coach and railway interchange.

The railway eventually reached Bournemouth in 1870, long after Poole, Dorchester and Weymouth had been put on the railway map. The population of the already fast-growing town simply took off. There were 6,000 inhabitants in 1871, and 17,000 ten years later.

Bournemouth did not exist at the beginning of the nineteenth century, but once the beneficial effects of its pines and its mild climate had been realized, it began its transformation into what it claims is the premier resort on the South Coast. Bournemouth has always seen itself as a cut above most other seaside towns although it has never quite gone to

Frinton's length of forbidding licensed premises within its frontiers. It gives no great welcome to day-trippers and excursion traffic has never formed a large part of passenger traffic on the Bournemouth line. The Waterloo to Bournemouth route became perhaps the most prestigious of the LSWR main lines and the Southern Railway continued this tradition, introducing the all-Pullman 'Bournemouth Belle', powered by 'Lord Nelson' and 'King Arthur' 4-6-0s, and the 'Schools'-hauled 'Bournemouth Limited' in the 1930s.

The Somerset & Dorset Joint Railway reached Bournemouth over its meandering single track line from Bath, and in LMS and early BR days a number of through trains from the Midlands and the North, notably the 'Pines Express', arrived in Bournemouth during the summer months. Bulleid 'Pacifics', the unique Derby-built Fowler 2-8-0s, '2P' 4-4-0s, Stanier and BR Standard 4-6-0s and '9F' 2-10-0s all brought enthusiasts flocking to the route in its last years.

The S&D — and its Bournemouth West station — closed in 1966, a year before the Waterloo to Bournemouth line was electrified. Although that event signified the end of the career of the Bulleid 'Pacifics', or so it seemed, a quite astonishing number have been preserved, and as I write seven have been restored to working order with others well on the way back to steam.

Hampshire and West Sussex

Having reached the Solent we have gained a part of the British Isles that was able to afford so many railway lines that it is a wonder there was any room for the pebbles. Whilst some of the lines between Southampton and the Thames Estuary are no longer with us, there remain more places along this part of our coastline with extant railway stations than any comparable stretch in the British Isles.

In the depths of the New Forest runs the

electrified Lymington branch, leaving the main line at Brockenhurst. This has excellent connections to Freshwater, the shortest crossing from the mainland to the Isle of Wight.

The Isle of Wight could once boast 34 stations. Now it has eight, and it was not so long ago that even these were threatened. By no means all were on the sea, but none was very far from it. The LSWR and the LB&SCR jointly served three, Pier head, Esplanade and St Johns in Ryde, the island's principal resort. There was once a tramway along the pier, but now the trains have a monopoly. All of Ryde's stations still exist and are served by ancient former London tube trains, the only self-propelled items of rolling-stock which can get through the narrow bore of the tunnel which takes the railway under eastern Ryde. The line, built by the Isle of Wight Railway in 1864, continues south past the site of Smallbrook Junction to Brading, Sandown and Shanklin. It used to extend further through Wroxall and through another tunnel to Ventnor on the south coast, but this section was closed in 1966 when the rest was

electrified. Sandown, Shanklin and Ryde are the most popular resorts on the island, hence the survival of their railway stations.

The rest of the Isle of Wight was served by the Isle of Wight Central Railway and the Freshwater, Yarmouth & Newport Railway, dating from 1866 and 1888 respectively. Neither was exactly prosperous and when the Southern Railway absorbed them in 1923 it got rid of their ancient, second-hand rolling-stock as soon as possible. There followed the heyday of the island railways, with neat, well-kept, spritely little tank engines and rakes of carefully maintained carriages. Holiday traffic boomed and by the late 1930s former LSWR '02' 0–4–4Ts and former LB&SCR 'E1' and 'Terrier' 0–6–0Ts handled all the passenger and goods traffic, whilst the carriages were pre-grouping bogie non-corridors. The Cowes-Newport-Smallbrook Junction line was

Stalwart of the Isle of Wight passenger services, '02' Class 0–4–4T No 23 *Totland* pauses between turns on Ryde Pier on a summer's day in the mid-1930s. (*Author's collection*)

A former London 'tube' train at Ryde in June 1984.

the second busiest, Cowes, of course, being a famous yachting centre whilst Newport is the island capital.

However, by the 1950s road traffic was eating into the railways' profits. By 1953 Merstone station, between Sandown and Newport, was no longer a junction, for the branch from there to Ventnor had gone the previous year, and at the end of that summer the only line in West Wight, from Newport to Freshwater, closed. Sitting on the beach at Bembridge that August, I watched an '02' in charge of the branch line train arrive from Brading; this too would close that summer. The Sandown-Newport line went in 1956, then there was a lull until the final closure, that of the Cowes to Ryde line in 1966.

Well — not a total closure. '02' No 24 *Calbourne* and six carriages, three of LB&SCR origin and three built by the SE&CR, were stored at Newport until 1971 when they moved to Havenstreet, three stations along the line to Ryde. That summer public services over the 1¾ miles to Wootton began. Since then, two Brighton-built 'Terriers' which worked on the Isle of Wight Central Railway and had, remarkably, survived on the mainland, have returned, whilst a fourth

engine regularly at work is a 1915–built Hawthorne Leslie 0-4-0ST from the Woolwich Arsenal. No locomotive or carriage on the Isle of Wight Steam Railway was built after 1924, a unique distinction amongst the British preservation scene. With the active encouragement of Network SouthEast, the steam railway is being extended to link up with BR at Smallbrook Junction.

Not the least enjoyable part of an Isle of Wight holiday is the crossing of the Solent. Great favourites on the Portsmouth-Ryde run were the *Southsea*, *Brading* and *Shanklin*, ferries ordered by the Southern Railway from Dennys on the Clyde immediately after the Second World War and in service until the 1980s. The *Ryde*, another Denny vessel, was the last survivor of a previous generation, a paddle-steamer built in 1939 and the last such to remain in service with Sealink.

Back on the mainland, the main line now approaches Southampton, and the Fawley branch comes in from the south. This was built by the Southern Railway in 1925, and although it lost its passenger service in 1966 it is still very busy with traffic to and from the great refinery. Next, the line from Romsey and Salisbury joins from the north-west, another busy route and becoming more so with 'Sprinters' working an hourly service to

Bristol. Swinging around the head of Southampton Water there is a clear view down the Western Docks, where, even now, an occasional liner may be seen, but more commonly a large container ship, often flying P&O colours.

Leaving the main station in Southampton, which is once again often unofficially called Central, the line tunnels under the city centre and the finest art gallery on the South Coast, swings sharply northwards at the other end, is joined by the single track down which *QE2* boat trains proceed to the docks past the now trackless but carefully restored Docks station, one-time terminus of GWR trains of the Didcot and Winchester line, and finds itself once again beside the water. The next station, St Denys, is one of the finest examples of pure Victoriana anywhere on British Rail, and its recent sensitive restoration and repainting was deservedly recognized by a major conservation award. The main line to London heads north-eastwards and inland, but we turn our attention to the coast route to Fareham and Portsmouth, presently in process of electrification.

Its rather slow and twisty but a pleasant line if one is not in a hurry. I had not realized just how attractive it could appear until returning from Gatwick Airport early on a Sunday morning last summer. The windows were opened wide and the scent of wild flowers, hay and, most aromatic of all, a distinctive mixture of seaweed, salt water and melting tar drifted in as we crossed the Hamble at Burlesdon.

A line from Fareham to Gosport was opened as long ago as 1841 and was sometimes used by Queen Victoria returning from Osborne House on the Isle of Wight. There was also a branch from Fort Brockhurst to Lee-on-the-Solent, which was to become a flying boat base in the early years of the present century. Passenger services to the latter ended in 1931 and to Gosport in 1953.

Portsmouth was the site of a major battle between the LSWR and the LB&SCR. Both got there in the 1840s, the Brighton winning the race in 1847, the South Western arriving

a year later. Trains finished up literally on top of the water at Portsmouth Harbour station whilst ¾ mile eastwards was Portsmouth and Southsea station, Southsea being where the beach and the funfair was, and is, found. The station here, with high and low levels, has recently been colourfully rebuilt.

The Waterloo to Portsmouth line was electrified in 1937, the multiple units which worked it being adorned with the headboards 'Waterloo, Portsmouth and the Isle of Wight'. This led to the not surprising assumption by the uninitiated that a train ferry was also part of the grand moderniza-

Portsmouth Harbour station, March 1989. The Victorian warship *Warrior* is seen through the station entrance.

tion scheme, and that one could board one's electric train in London, sail in it across the Solent and alight wherever one chose on the Isle of Wight. In 1938 the rival former Brighton line route, the Mid-Sussex, by way of Horsham, Arundel and Chichester was also electrified. The Waterloo line was always the faster and nowadays is the only realistic choice, for the Mid-Sussex line has been downgraded and trains between London Bridge, Victoria and Portsmouth come down the main line to Preston Park and then head along the coast through Hove so that they can no longer be regarded as expresses. The fast trains to Waterloo take $1\frac{1}{2}$ hours from Portsmouth Harbour — to Victoria they take 2 hours 11 minutes.

Included in the Mid-Sussex electrification scheme was the Bognor Regis branch. Bognor, like many South Coast resorts, owed much to royal patronage and it acquired its suffix by courtesy of King George V who convalesced there in 1928, although the first royal visitor had been Princess Charlotte, granddaughter of George III, who spent the summers of 1808–10 in the town. Bognor station is distinctly above average with a rather nice booking hall, and plenty of well-cared-for ironwork and glass. Semaphore signals can still be found there; the combination of Southern electrics and semaphores which was once so common is now only to be found on this part of the Sussex coast and is not likely to last much longer.

In the days immediately after Dunkirk, invasion was a real possibility, and one could not visit the coast without permission, so the holiday and day-tripper business had ceased. Private motoring had, too, and there was a vast amount of military comings and goings, so the railways, despite the absence of holiday traffic, were very busy. For the Mid-Sussex electric express units Bulleid had designed some very avant-garde buffet cars but such luxuries had been banished for the duration.

The antiquarian enthusiast should on no account miss Pagham beach, some three miles west of Bognor pier. Here is probably the largest collection of old railway carriage chalet homes in Britain. There are dozens of them, 'Rhodina', 'Bijou', 'The Moorings', some instantly recognizable with drop lights, door handles, ventilator louvres and even the occasional engraved 'Smoking' sign on the glass still intact. Others, pebble-dashed perhaps, or much hacked around and incorporated into a larger building, are only detectable by a telltale tumblehome or a regular window pattern.

Two form part of the clubhouse of the Pagham Yacht Club. The barman told me that they had been brought from Barnham Junction by horse 'some time around 1900–1910, the West Sussex Railway, does that sound right?' In fact, although the first owners of old railway carriage homes are often very difficult to determine, some of the Pagham ones instantly betray their Stroudley LB&SCR origins by their distinctive guard's lookouts, one at least still with its end windows, which must have been looking out over the English Channel for some 70 years, far longer than they viewed the various parts of Surrey and Sussex which the four-wheel passenger brake to which they belong would have trundled round during the last decades of the nineteenth century.

Between Portsmouth and Bognor there were two other seaside lines. One was the LB&SCR branch from Havant to Hayling Island. Opened in 1867, it lasted until 1963 and was celebrated for having been worked by 'Terriers' for something like 80 years. The other was one of Colonel Stephens' light railways and ran from Chichester down the Selsey Peninsula to the sea. It liked to be called the Hundred of Manhood & Selsey Tramways or, later, the West Sussex Railway, which sounded very grand indeed. It was nothing of the sort, of course. It opened in 1897, with a siding connection to the LB&SCR, did quite well for a while, then, after the First World War, when vast numbers of war surplus motor vehicles were let loose upon the roads, it went into an inevitable decline and eventually expired in 1935.

Where it all began

Next we come to Littlehampton. The London, Brighton & South Coast Railway reached it in 1863, a year before its neighbour, Bognor. There is a triangular junction beside the Arun so trains can run direct to the town from both east and west. Littlehampton is an unpretentious little town with a harbour with houseboats, a few yachts, a couple of coasters, a boat yard, a museum constructed partly out of ships' timbers, a long promenade, a big fun-fair and a Brighton 'Atlantic' painted on the pub sign beside the newly rebuilt and greatly improved station in the town centre, hard by the Arun. There's an excellent hourly service to London, the four-car CIG unit joining up with the Portsmouth section at Worthing and taking an hour and a half, and hourly coastal stopping trains to Portsmouth and Brighton with connections at Ford for the Mid-Sussex line.

There are no more seaside branch lines now, living or dead, until Brighton, for the main line runs very close to the sea, although it is not until Shoreham that passengers actually get a sight of it, since the land is so flat.

Greenhouses border the line on either side, whence boxes of carnations and other flowers used to come up by train to Victoria, but the road has the monopoly now. Angmering, Goring-by-Sea and Durrington serve many square miles of neat estates of retirement bungalows, whilst Worthing, which boasts no fewer than three stations, has a rather more cosmopolitan clientele, including at least 200 homeless families housed in bed and breakfast accommodation.

The station is a handsome, typically late-nineteenth-century LB&SCR structure with lots of fancy ironwork. There is an EMU depot at West Worthing, but nothing remains of the former carriage works at Lancing, the next station up the line from East Worthing. West Worthing is the terminus of a suburban service from Brighton, electrified at the same time as the London to Brighton line in 1932, and originally served by elderly former LSWR London suburban units and specially converted but equally elderly 2NOLs. Just before the long bridge over the Adur estuary,

A 'Gladstone' 0–4–2 crosses the Adur estuary at Shoreham with a westbound train of Stroudley four-wheelers, *circa* 1890. (*Author's collection*)

Brighton station in the spring of 1988 with Electro-diesel No 73101 on a train from Exeter and EMU No 319023 just arrived from Bedford.

which is almost all mud at low tide, the railway runs alongside Shoreham airport whose terminal building is a fine example of 1930s 'streamline' architecture, a style employed on a number of houses and parades of shops in this part of the South Coast.

The Shoreham to Brighton line was the very first section of railway on the south coast, being opened in 1840. Shoreham is a port, quite a busy one for both cargo and pleasure craft, hence its early appearance on the rail map of these islands. Much of the material needed for building the London to Brighton line arrived at Shoreham; nowadays very little cargo between towns and cities in England and Wales travels by water, but 150 years ago very little of it did not.

A surprising number of passengers also travelled this way and there was a regular steam packet between London and various south coast towns. It took 13 hours to sail the 160 miles from Greenwich to Brighton, and three hours from Hastings. Passengers embarked and disembarked at the pier, especially built for the purpose and of a most interesting construction, slung by chains from posts driven into the sea bed, hence its title 'The Chain Pier'.

The line east of Shoreham station runs within a few yards of the harbour, divided from it by warehouses, but no longer serves it. A branch from Horsham, Christs Hospital and Steyning used to run along the eastern bank of the Adur to Shoreham, providing one of many alternative routes between London and Brighton. It closed to passenger traffic in 1966. Freight from the cement works beneath the downs at Beeding lasted a while longer

but that too has now ceased.

Brighton probably has the best claim to the title 'World's First Seaside Resort' though others, not least Scarborough, get very cross about this and dispute it strongly. What is certain is that by 1830 it had a population of over 40,000 and was the favourite with the leaders of fashion, the Court and the smart set; in other words, if you considered yourself anyone at all, you made jolly sure you were seen taking the waters at Brighton. Naturally enough, anywhere so avant-garde had to possess whatever was the latest, so a bill to build a railway line from London to Brighton passed through Parliament in 1837, within a month of Queen Victoria's coronation. Her Majesty possessed a palace at Brighton, the Royal Pavilion, the creation of her uncle, George IV. With the completion of the railway in 1841, the Queen often travelled down to Brighton by train although she did not entirely desert the royal yacht. However, everyone else also started coming to Brighton too. This the Queen did not like. The place became vulgar, so she fled across the water to the seclusion of Osborne on the Isle of Wight. The LB&SCR was not bothered, for vast hordes of the vulgar, as well as considerable quantities of the refined, found Brighton just the thing and came down for the day or longer.

Brighton grew and grew and its station grew with it. The original, serving the Shoreham line, was fairly unimpressive, but very

shortly afterwards the company's architect David Moccatta gave the town a magnificent structure, erected on a curving site cut into a hillside ten minutes walk from the seafront which, although enlarged in the 1880s, remains today essentially as he planned it. Other seaside towns acquired fine stations, many of which have either been demolished, reduced in importance or put to other uses, but Brighton station, sensitively modernized and recently repainted, is busier than ever. It is without equal, the finest piece of seaside railway architecture in the land.

That epitome of luxurious travel, the Pullman car, was more closely associated with the Brighton line than any other. The first complete Pullman train in the British Isles took up work between Victoria station and Brighton in 1881 and more and more Pullmans appeared on the LB&SCR until the position was reached when most Sussex coast expresses included at least one. When the Brighton line was electrified in 1932, each six-car express EMU included a Pullman whilst three five-car units of Pullmans were built to work the 'Southern Belle', shortly to be renamed the 'Brighton Belle'. By this time Brighton was frequently called 'London-by-the-sea' and any young female inhabitant of prepossessing aspect was likely to be referred to as a 'Brighton Belle'. The Pullman Car Company established its works at Preston Park beside the junction of the Brighton and the West Coast lines. Sadly, despite the revival of Pullman travel on the BR network in the 1980s, none are now normally seen working on the Brighton line, but there is considerable compensation in that the works is now the home of several preservation groups and a number of Pullmans, both from the 'Brighton Belle' and of much earlier origin, are being restored there. The locomotive works of the LB&SCR went into decline in early Southern Railway days, reviv-

Brighton as seen by 'The Road to Sunshine', the Southern Railway.

FAME. **BRIGHTON** FASHION.

ILLUSTRATED GUIDE, PROGRAMME OF EVENTS & ACCOMMODATION LIST FROM CORPORATION PUBLICITY DEPT. BRIGHTON.

THE ROAD TO SOUTHERN RAILWAY

SIXTY-MINUTE PULLMAN EXPRESSES FROM LONDON. THROUGH TRAINS FROM WEST, NORTH AND MIDLANDS.

ed dramatically during the 1940s to the extent that large numbers of Bulleid 'Pacifics' were built there, and then, after nationalisation, built several series of the handsome and very successful BR Standard 2–6–4Ts. Nothing now remains of the works but many of the locomotives which were built there have survived, on the Bluebell Railway and on many other preserved railways and in museums.

East from Brighton

The line east from Brighton curves away immediately beyond the station, as does the line to the west, but whilst the latter dives into a tunnel, the former crosses a most impressive viaduct which carries it across the valley through which runs the London Road. The extensive carriage depot at Lovers Walk lies beside the main line and provides much of the rolling-stock and many of the crews for the services radiating from Brighton.

A branch line totally contained within the borough of Brighton served Kemp Town. It was worked by some curious appliances, steam motors and battery cars for example, but none could successfully compete with the more direct trams and buses and it closed to passengers in 1932, although the odd special penetrated the tunnel, in which most of the line was contained, until its demise in 1970.

At Lewes, the ancient, hilly, county town of East Sussex, the line from Brighton joins the London to Eastbourne line. Lewes station is extensive and busy. Immediately to the east, the lines to Sheffield Park and East Grinstead, to Uckfield, Tunbridge Wells and Oxted used to diverge, and a bit further on that to Newhaven and Seaford still does. This runs along the eastern banks of the Ouse, past Virginia Woolf's last home, to the sea.

The Newhaven-Dieppe route between London and Paris involved a longer sea voyage than that across the Channel from either

The 'Southern Belle' leaving Victoria for Brighton in the charge of an LB&SCR 4–6–4T in about 1922. (*Author's collection*)

Right The all-electric 'Brighton Belle' heading south along the Quarry line, *circa* 1937. (*Author's collection*)

Below One of the prototype express 4CEP units at Brighton in January 1979.

Folkestone or Dover, but was rather cheaper and was therefore always popular with students and other impecunious souls. The sea off Newhaven is notorious for working itself into a tremendous fury, and the LB&SCR built a breakwater 1,000 yards long to protect shipping entering and leaving.

Newhaven's one really grand hotel, the London and Paris, another railway enterprise, was demolished a good few years ago, having outlived its usefulness. Until the 1970s, even after steam had gone, the Newhaven boat train was locomotive hauled, latterly by Class '73s', but nowadays it is made up of EMUs and is in no way distinctive. A famous resident of the town for many years was — no, not the last French king, Louis Phillipe, he stayed at the Bridge in the middle of the town after being deposed in 1848 — but No 72, the very first of the celebrated Stroudley 'Terrier' tank engines.

No 72 *Fenchurch* was built in 1872 and 26 years later was sold to the Newhaven Harbour Company. She was taken over by the Southern Railway in 1927 and continued to trundle up and down the quayside for no

fewer than 65 years. When withdrawn in 1963 at the age of 91 she had been the oldest locomotive on British Railways for 13 years. Naturally so remarkable a veteran could not be sent off to the scrap heap, and today No 72 can be found at work on the Bluebell Railway, still bearing the legend, on one side. 'Newhaven Harbour Company'.

Seaford gets an even worse battering from the sea than Newhaven, and it can toss pebbles high over the tops of four and five storey hotels on the front. The railway lies a few hundred yards back and is thus reasonably secure. Having reached Newhaven in 1847, the railway arrived at Seaford 17 years later. It could go no further, for the town is set hard against Seaford Head and from here eastwards is a succession of high cliffs, the Seven Sisters, culminating in Beachy Head.

Incidentally, the famous Brighton 'Atlantic' No 32424 *Beachy Head* outlived all other 'Atlantics' on British Railways. I watched her steam past Norbury on a sunny spring morning in 1958 on her way from Victoria to Newhaven for the very last time hauling 'The

Sussex Coast Limited' special, a spendid sight. The LNWR-style lined black livery which adorned the Brighton 'Atlantics' in their final years was always kept clean and suited them very well. Eleven days later *Beachy Head* steamed off to Eastleigh to meet her end.

Beachy Head is within the borough of Eastbourne and in days of yore the Southdown bus company did much business transporting visitors from the railway station and other parts of the town to its 534 ft heights. I met my wife at Eastbourne, which I mention just to ensure that the reader realizes that there is absolutely no chance of my being objective about the place.

Eastbourne was very much the creation of the Dukes of Devonshire. When the railway arrived in 1849, its rapid growth was only just beginning and a rather grander, Gallic-influenced station became necessary in 1866.

Newhaven Harbour in 1970 with the last railway-owned paddle-steamer, the former Southern Railway *Ryde*, built by Dennys in 1937.

2BIL No 2075 about to leave Seaford for Haywards Heath on 4 October 1969.

This is the one still in use today. Electrification came in 1935 and the town has always enjoyed an excellent service to London. Currently the 61¾-mile journey takes 1 hour 20 minutes with stops at Clapham Junction, East Croydon, Gatwick Airport, Haywards Heath, Lewes and Polegate. Trains run every hour and continue on to Hastings and Ore, leaving a portion at Eastbourne.

Eastbourne is quite the cleanest town I know. There has long been rivalry with Brighton, and whilst I once used to think Eastbourne pretty dull by comparison, it is the sort of place which as one gets to know well one comes to appreciate. There are many fine Victorian and Edwardian villas, terraces and houses and it has grown rapidly since the 1970s, both inland and eastwards over the Crumbles, a once empty expanse along the shore, deserted save by a rich variety of seabirds.

Although always regarded by the LB&SCR as its exclusive territory, the South Eastern Railway made a foray towards Eastbourne in

1880 when a through route was opened by way of the Oxted line, Heathfield, Hailsham and Polegate. The SER put on two expresses in each direction between Charing Cross and Eastbourne but so few availed themselves of this unique opportunity that within a year they had vanished. From then on, the best

A 2BIL forming the 15.12 Ore to Brighton passing Pevensey Castle, June 1969.

that could be offered was a connecting service at Tunbridge Wells. This route came to be known as the Cuckoo Line, for legend had it that the first cuckoo of the year was always heard on Heathfield Fair Day, 14 April.

SECR 4-4-0s and 0-4-4Ts and 'birdcage' three-car non-corridor sets worked much of the services on the Tunbridge Wells to Eastbourne line until BR Standard 2-6-4Ts and Maunsell and Bulleid corridor stock ousted them. Eastbourne shed housed a collection of veterans around the time of nationalisation, including some of the despised 'I1X' 4-4-2Ts as well as the very fine 'I3s'. In the mid-1930s, Billinton's splendid 'Baltic' tanks had ended their days on the former LB&SCR system as the principal motive power for the London expresses; with electrification they were rebuilt at Eastleigh as 'N15X' Class 4-6-0s, and although they lasted in this form until the mid-1950s, they never recaptured the glories of their heyday.

The misguided Dr Beeching, faithfully following his misguided Government directive, closed first the Heathfield line as far south as Hailsham and then, at the end of 1968, the Hailsham to Polegate section. It was a most unnecessary closure — Hailsham

was expanding rapidly and was making increasing use of its diesel-electric multiple units.

Eastbourne has long been a popular resort with the elderly and through trains from various parts of the Midlands and the North were well patronized into the 1970s but, sadly, have now disappeared. Good connections may exist, but there is nothing like a through service, even if it is not especially fast.

East Sussex, West Kent

The line from Polegate and Eastbourne cuts behind the South Downs and passes along the edge of the Pevensey Levels or marshes which reach almost to the sea. It was here that William of Normandy landed and, some 1,900 years later, a small resort sprang up chiefly because of the presence of the railway. The village of Pevensey, dominated by its magnificent Norman castle, last used by the military in the Second World War, remains

Holidaymakers arriving at Eastbourne, July 1972.

unspoilt whilst it is possible to wander for half a day along the marsh roads, sometimes within sight of Pevensey Bay or Bexhill, and encounter no more than half a dozen vehicles and pass less than half that number of dwellings. The principal inhabitants of the marshes are sheep, cattle and birds. From Pevensey through Norman's Bay to Bexhill the narrow strip of land between the railway line and the sea has largely been given over to chalets and caravans, but behind it is one of the few, precious undeveloped areas on the Sussex coast.

Bexhill, St Leonards and Hastings were border country fought over by the LB&SCR and the SER. The former's coast line got to Bexhill in 1846, the SER, with a branch from its London to Hastings main line, very much later in 1902. This closed, after dieselization, in 1964, and the former LB&SCR station, rebuilt at the turn of the century, is now the only one in the town. For many years the Southern Railway featured the futuristic De La Warr Pavilion, built in 1936, on its posters; it is a fine piece of architecture, ideally situated, affording splendid views across the sea.

Hastings station dates from the same period, a reinforced concrete building of two island platforms, completed in 1931. Of course the railway was here long before that, the LB&SCR reaching the town in 1846, the SER five years later. The latter company, to make up for being second, approached Hastings from two directions, arriving from Ashford in 1851 and from Tonbridge in 1852. The latter line connected with the LB&SCR at the charmingly named Bopeep Junction, trains then coming to a halt at the resonant St Leonards Warrior Square. There are five tunnels in something like four miles between Bopeep Junction and Ore, the next station east of Hastings, which gives some idea of how hilly the twin towns of Hastings and St Leonards are. Despite the expense and difficulty these caused, the SER and the LB&SCR fought each other fiercely to gain the ascendancy. The result was a draw, and to this day there are hourly expresses between

Hastings and London over each of the rival routes. The former LB&SCR route to Victoria takes 1 hour 50 minutes, the SER to Charing Cross exactly an hour and a half. Electric trains have been running to Victoria since 1935, but the Charing Cross line was not electrified until the 1980s. Its trains wore a distinctive 'jaffa cake' livery of orange and brown for a time.

The SER route has long been noted for its unique rolling-stock. The narrowness of its tunnels resulted in Maunsell building some especially narrow versions of his standard corridor stock and, notably, his magnificent 'Schools' Class 4–4–0s. They proved to be such splendid movers that many more were built for service all over the Southern system. Regarded with a good deal less affection, at least in their early days, were the slab-sided DEMUs which replaced the 'Schools' in 1957. These were very noisy but quite comfortable and came out as six-car units. They lost their buffet cars in the 1970s through not being sufficiently well patronized, but refreshment facilities returned with electrification. Very right and proper too, for it's a most attractive route and is best appreciated with a cup of tea or coffee to hand.

As late as February 1956, the entire original batch of the first eleven of the 'Schools' Class was shedded at St Leonards, as it always had been. The 'Terriers' which worked the Kent & East Sussex Railway also lived there. In diesel days a depot for the DEMUs was set up, and this serviced the Oxted line units as well, despite the long detour this entailed down the Brighton main line and along the coast — the SER route from Tunbridge Wells through Battle would have been more direct but the tunnel restrictions prevented this. A batch of narrow-bodied Class '33' diesel locomotives — the 'Slim Jims' — was also built for the Hastings line. The problem was finally solved when the offending section was singled so that standard electric stock could be used.

There was a time, back in the 1960s, when the future of the Ashford to Hastings line, a useful link between Sussex and the Kent coast

THE SOUTH COAST

Left Stalwart of the Brighton line semi-fast and stopping services for over 35 years, and the only 4LAV to receive all-yellow ends, No 2950 awaits its end at Polegate, June 1969.

Right RH&DR 'Pacific' No 8 *Hurricane* at New Romney, May 1989.

ports, was very much under threat, but the prospects of the Channel Tunnel helped save it, plus some very effective campaigning by the locals who travelled on it.

Winchelsea and the quite remarkably picturesque Cinque Port of Rye were once on the sea, but the rest of the journey is inland. Passenger trains used to take the branch from Appledore to Dungeness and Romney, but now it only sees freight connected with the nuclear power station built on the edge of the sea.

Nevertheless, passenger trains, and steam-hauled ones at that, still run to Dungeness on what is billed as 'The World's Smallest Public Railway', the Romney, Hythe & Dymchurch. When I first knew the line immediately after the Second World War, with its miniature Gresley-type 'Pacifics' and 4-8-2s, it was quite something. The creation of a racing-car driver, Captain Howey, and the engineer Henry Greenly, the railway had, and still has, very much the air of a scaled down main line. Hythe station had an overall roof and the line from there to New Romney was double track, whilst New Romney itself, the hub of the system, with its locomotive and carriage depots and works, had something of a Swin-

don or Crewe about it. Chalets and caravans between the railway and the sea provided plenty of business all along the line between Hythe and New Romney, and inland stretched the marshes populated by sheep and legends of smugglers and revenue men. My father took my picture standing beside *Dr Syn*, a Canadian Pacific type 4-6-2 named after the most famous of the marsh smugglers, when our train drew into Dungeness, a desolate, shingle-strewn headland dominated by its lighthouse. The nuclear power station would come later.

In the 1940s and '50s there were more than enough holidaymakers in this part of Kent to keep the railway busy, but the affluent '60s saw changing times and for many years now, through several changes of ownership, there have been threats, or promises, depending upon how one views the situation, to uproot the Romney, Hythe & Dymchurch and take it elsewhere.

There used to be a branch off the Ashford to Folkestone main line to Hythe and Sandgate. It closed in 1931 and the RH&DR had plans to extend from Hythe to the Southern main line, and even went so far as to build two 4-8-2s to cope with the gradients, but the

line was never built, and when we went off to look at the cross-Channel boats at Folkestone we took a cherry-red East Kent double-deck bus.

Continental connections

Folkestone and Dover have long been inextricably linked and seen as twin ports through which most of the traffic between England and the Continent passes, but Folkestone has, from the early nineteenth century, also been very much a resort, and for a while quite a fashionable one. Today Folkestone is in the centre of the construction of what may well be about the greatest revolution in rail travel this century, the long-awaited Channel Tunnel. When that opens travel to the seaside will take on a whole new dimension.

The South Eastern Railway very nearly got to Folkestone by the summer of 1843. However, it came to an abrupt halt on the western edge of the town for it was confronted by a deep valley and had to wait for the 19-arch viaduct spanning it to be completed at the end of the year. This done, a station was

opened beyond the viaduct and a line was constructed which descended precipitously down to the harbour. The history of Folkestone and its stations is complicated. A station was opened on the western side of the viaduct which became known as Folkestone Central, though it hasn't always been called that, and another one, west again, became the West station, although it was once Shorncliffe Camp, there being a very large military camp here. The original, junction, station eventually closed down in the 1960s.

The SER went to some lengths to develop the harbour and in 1849 the steamer service began to Boulogne. Folkestone, however, was much more than a ferry port. It became a resort of the first rank. Even today, the cumulative magnificence and elegance achieved by the conglomeration of brick, stone, terracotta, iron and glass which the Victorian and Edwardian builders and architects employed in the avenues of tree-lined, lawn-and-flowerbed-encompassed hotels on the Leas, the high cliffs of western Folkestone, is breathtaking.

The elegant Edwardian ladies and gentlemen who stayed at Folkestone and who promenaded in all their finery along the Leas, gazing out across the Channel to France, would have come down from London behind Harry Wainwright's equally elegant deep-green-liveried 4–4–0s, travelling in brown-painted 'birdcage' non-corridor carriages, or, more likely, a crimson and gold Pullman. Later, the more powerful German-built 'L' Class and then their Southern Railway successors, the 'L1s', had charge of the 'Folkestone Limited'.

The harbour line has long provided a fascinating spectacle as trains struggle up it, and in steam days three 0–6–0Ts were often employed, usually Stirling 'R' and 'R1' Class, whilst one could reckon on coming upon at least one of the little Wainwright 'P' Class 0–6–0Ts shunting along the quay. Nowadays only the Orient Express regularly uses the harbour line, connections from the Sealink boats being 'by bus to the town station', which is a great inconvenience for passengers. Perhaps with the imminence of the Channel Tunnel, ferry passengers are considered dispensable.

The Channel Tunnel will bring about a completely new dimension to travel to the sea, not least because passengers won't actually ever see — barring accidents — any of it. As the £1½ million centre at Folkestone beside the site for the terminal informs the visitor, the journey time from London to Paris by rail will be 2 hours 40 minutes, which is 20 minutes less than the present city centre to city centre flying time. Just think of it. If British Rail get it right — there's no fear that SNCF and the French will miss out — the Channel Tunnel will give the biggest boost to passenger and rail travel in Britain since George Stephenson opened the Liverpool & Manchester Railway. One will miss the delights of the sea crossing — in good weather — though not the primitive conditions of getting on and off the boats, and it is to be hoped that all those in Folkestone and more especially Dover who depend on the ferries for their livelihood will find alternative work with the Tunnel company. One feels rather less sympathy with the majority of those campaigning against the rail route

through Kent. Leaving aside the fact that much of their criticism is ill-informed, the nub of the matter is surely that environmentally an electric railway is far and away preferable to ever increasing motor traffic clogging the roads leading to the Channel ports.

The line across the viaduct at Folkestone continued on to Dover, which was reached in 1844. At the other end of the town the Elham Valley line, opened in 1889, came in from Canterbury. Never more than a fairly sleepy branch line, the Southern Railway closed it in 1940. The 7½-mile line to Dover is one of the best-known stretches of railway in the country, running as it does along the foot of, and in places through, the famous white cliffs.

British Railways introduced a Pullman train to the Kent coast, the 'Thanet Belle', later renamed the 'Kentish Belle', but much more famous was the 'Golden Arrow'. This originated on the French side of the Channel in 1926 as the 'Flèche d'Or', operated by the Nord company; three years later the 'Golden Arrow' name was bestowed on the English connecting service. Normally worked to and from Dover by locomotives of the 'Lord Nelson' Class, after its restoration in 1946 Bulleid 'Pacifics' took over, bearing gold arrows and the French and British flags. Its most famous period was from 1951, when two British Railways-designed 'Britannia' 'Pacifics', Nos 70004 *William Shakespeare* (which had been exhibited at the Festival of Britain) and 70014 *Iron Duke* were especially allocated to work it. Kept in superb condition by Stewarts Lane, the handsome 'Pacifics' with their rake of beautiful chocolate and cream Pullmans, built at the same time, provided a splendid spectacle. By the late 1950s air travel was taking away much of the 'Arrow's' most prestigious clientele, and although it survived into electric days it had little to distinguish it at the end, most of its carriages being ordinary vehicles, the three or four surviving Pullmans being repainted in corporate and highly inappropriate blue and grey livery. It ceased altogether in September 1972.

That, however, was not the end of the

story, for James B. Sherwood, the American President of the Sea Containers Group and buyer of Sealink from British Rail, decided that the 1980s was a fit time for a revival of Pullman travel. As is well known, he spent millions buying and restoring old Pullmans and Wagons-Lits on both sides of the Channel and now once again it is possible to travel in the height of luxury — if one can afford it — down to the sea from Victoria, cross the Channel from Folkestone, and then head south-eastwards through France and Switzerland to Venice.

When the Southern Region set about extending electrification to the Kent Coast it decided to opt for EMUs. In this it was following a long-established tradition. The units, although of BR Mark 1 design, were basically updated versions of the Portsmouth and Mid-Sussex stock introduced in the late 1930s. The prototypes appeared in 1956 and ran extensive trials on the Central Section and, indeed, spent all their working lives there until rebuilt in the 1980s. Designated 4CEPs and 4BEPs (the buffet car versions), the production sets took up regular work on

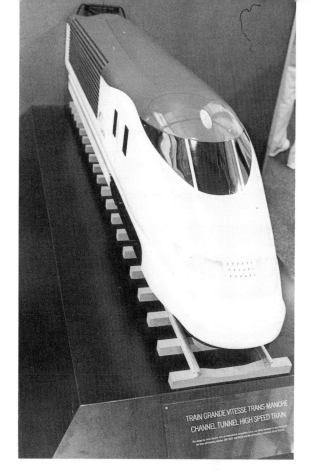

Above   Model of a Channel Tunnel High Speed Train.

Below   No 21C57 *Biggin Hill* with the down 'Thanet Belle' in the summer of 1948. (*E.R. Wethersett*)

FOLKESTONE WARREN & DOVER CLIFFS.
SOUTH EASTERN & CHATHAM RAILWAY.

Left A SECR 'E' Class 4-4-0 with a London express at Folkestone Warren, *circa* 1910. (*Author's collection*)

Right Up and down 'Flèche D'Or' passing at Boulogne in September 1967. The up train approaching is in charge of Chapelon rebuilt 'Pacific' No 231K31.

Below right Bulleid 'Pacific' No 21C133 *Chard* leaving Victoria with the down 'Golden Arrow' in June 1947. (*Author's collection*)

15 June 1959, replacing steam on both boat trains and ordinary express workings. Gone were Pullmans, except on the 'Golden Arrow', and the great variety of coaching stock, ranging from 50-year-old SECR non-corridor sets to BR standard corridors, little different from the replacing EMUs. The long-familiar 'birdcage' sets disappeared almost overnight, although several such carriages would eventually end up on the Bluebell and Kent & East Sussex Railways. Green remained the livery, but the only locomotive-hauled boat trains left were the 'Night Ferry' and the 'Golden Arrow', both the responsibility of the striking-looking but not wildly successful Class '71' Co-Co electrics.

The first 14 of these came out of Doncaster works in 1959, an unusual birthplace for Southern Electrics; the remaining ten arrived a year later. The 'Night Ferry', with its Wagons-Lits sleepers, was perhaps the most distinctive train operating on the British Railways network. Running each night from London to Paris and Brussels, the brown-uniformed attendants who conducted passengers to their berths at Victoria station performed their duties with a flourishing debonair deference which never failed to

make one feel one was already half-way across the Channel and anticipating that marvellous early morning arrival at the Gare du Nord past the white dome of Sacre Coeur looking down on the tracks from the heights of Montmartre.

The South Eastern and the London, Chatham & Dover railways fought tooth and nail for the lucrative traffic at Dover, Britain's principal cross-Channel port. The SER got there first in 1844, from London Bridge by way of Redhill, Tonbridge, Ashford and Folkestone; its rival, from Victoria, Chatham and Canterbury, took 17 years longer. Apart from the Marine or Western Docks station there is Priory, which serves the town, north of which, beyond two short tunnels, the Canterbury and the coast lines diverge.

Dover, unlike Folkestone, has never laid any claim to be a resort, but the coast line serves several small seaside holiday towns — Walmer, Deal and Sandwich — and also a coal mine, Betteshanger, one of several in east Kent. The LC&DR reached Deal in 1847 from Canterbury West and Minster, but it was not until 1881 that the SER and the LC&DR, realizing that excessive competition was crippling them both, agreed to the link

from Deal to Dover.

Minster boasts a triangular junction. Trains proceeding along the coast generally take the east curve and thus miss the station, although the odd ones reverse in and out. Most of the trains calling at Minster are on their way to or from Ramsgate, five minutes away. Ramsgate and its twin, Margate, are the most popular of all the many Kent coast resorts. The railway did wonders for them both, though it certainly did not create them, for they were already quite busy ports. The Duke of Wellington set off to deal with Napoleon from Ramsgate, whilst Margate was equally important militarily and was also a great haven for smugglers.

It was the Thames steamers which really turned Margate and Ramsgate into resorts. The first successful commercial steamer, the *Comet* was launched on the Clyde in 1812 and by 1815 there were four at work on the Thames, all Glasgow built. Since Margate lies on the north-easterly tip of Kent and is, strictly speaking, in the Thames Estuary, it was a natural destination for the steamers which, by the 1820s, were carrying many thousands of passengers. Ramsgate was too far for day-trippers in the early years, but as the steamers grew larger and faster — there were 17 by 1830 — it became possible to set off from Tower Pier early in the morning and have several hours ashore at Margate or rather less at Ramsgate.

The arrival of the South Eastern Railway at the two resorts in 1846 soon brought to an end the all-year-round steamer passenger services, but a summertime cruise down the river to the Kent coast remained immensely popular with Londoners until after the Second World War. We shall return to the steamers, and particularly the famous Eagle paddlers of the General Steam Navigation Co, when we cross the Thames to have a look at Southend.

The SER station at Ramsgate Town was a terminus, so trains continuing on to Margate Sands had to reverse out. The LC&DR, arriving 17 years later, built through stations at Margate West and East and a terminus at Ramsgate Sands, the latter reached by a tunnel. It also opened a station between Margate and Ramsgate at Broadstairs, yet another port which was to develop into a resort. Broadstairs station consists of two platforms, within sight of the sea, adjacent to the bowling green and next door to a museum devoted to Crampton, the designer of, amongst other things, some of the earliest locomotives to serve the Kent coast.

Throughout the last century all three resorts grew and grew as the trippers and holidaymakers poured in. The trains from London, whether by way of Ashford or the Medway towns, were not particularly fast and the carriages of both the SER and the LC&DR were notoriously amongst the most primitive and uncomfortable in the country, but it didn't matter — the journey was less than 80 miles and it was worth it for a day on the sands. The electric trains which provide an excellent service today, although 30 years old and not the smoothest-riding BR stock, were refurbished in the early 1980s and are a

Left The 'Orient Express' and the Sealink ferry *Horsa* at Boulogne, May 1987.

Right Greenwich Pier *circa* 1900. (*Author's collection*)

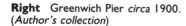

Below Ramsgate Harbour station in South Eastern days. (*Author's collection*)

deal more comfortable than anything the SER and LC&DR ever thought to offer the ordinary passenger.

With the Grouping, the Southern Railway quickly decided to simplify the complications of the Thanet coast network. The SER route between Margate and Ramsgate disappeared, as did both Margate Sands and Ramsgate Sands stations. New stations were provided in both towns, Ramsgate getting a through one for the first time, which was very jolly for the operating authorities but not half so convenient for the customers. Ramsgate became the principal engine shed in the area and the latest engines were usually stationed there, although bridges had to be strengthened by

the Southern Railway at various places on the main line before 4–6–0s could be introduced. Although Ramsgate had ten 'King Arthurs' in 1939 and many others of the class were regular visitors from Stewarts Lane, Dover and elsewhere, 4–4–0s were associated with the Ramsgate and Margate expresses until the very end of steam, despite the advent of large numbers of Bulleid 'Pacifics' after the Second World War.

Thanet, Thames and Medway

Westwards along the Thames estuary coast from Margate stretches a succession of small seaside towns and villages, many with stations, Westgate-on-Sea, Birchington-on-Sea, Herne Bay and, finally, Whitstable. The latter was served, not only by the London, Chatham & Dover's main line, but also by a direct line to Canterbury.

The Canterbury & Whitstable is virtually a prehistoric railway, quite the oldest in all southern England. It opened in 1830. Robert Stephenson built its engines and the first of these, *Invicta*, a four-wheeler, was most far-sightedly preserved by the SER at Ashford Works in 1853. Later it was put on display beside the city walls at Canterbury; presently it resides at the Poor Priest Hospital in the city. The Canterbury & Whitstable Railway

Charing Cross on 20 August 1932; 'B1' 4–4–0 No 457 with the 2.53 pm to Maidstone, and 'D1' 4–4–0 No 1479 with the 2.27 pm to Margate. (*Madgwick*)

actually opened four months before the Liverpool & Manchester, on 3 May 1830, and *Invicta* was thus the first locomotive in the world to haul regular passenger trains. Not for very long though, as the good burgers of Whitstable considered steam would never catch on and replaced *Invicta* with horses before the decade was out, steam working only the 1¼ miles of level track at the Whitstable end, the rest being cable operated. Eventually steam returned, although because of a low bridge under the main coast route only locomotives with cut-down boiler mountings and cabs — Stirling 'R1' tanks — could work down to the harbour. Passenger traffic ended on the Canterbury & Whitstable in 1931 and goods at the beginning of 1953.

The Isle of Sheppey, set on the south side of the Thames Estuary opposite Southend and Shoeburyness, is separated from the rest of Kent by the River Swale. The railway arrived in 1860 running from Sittingbourne on the main LC&DR North Kent line across the island to Queenborough and Sheerness-on-Sea on the north coast. Later, a line was constructed to a pier at Queenborough and a steamer service ran from there for many years to the Belgian port of Flushing. The Sheppey Light Railway opened in the summer of 1901, from Queenborough across to the eastern

shore at Leysdown. Operated by the LC&DR and its successors, it closed in 1950. ·
Sheerness, and much of the western side of the island, are heavily industrial with docks, shipyards, paper mills and steel works, although the town possesses a mile long sand and shingle beach. The Sheerness line was electrified along with the main line in 1959.

Exploration further west, past where the River Medway joins the Thames, brings us to the Medway Towns. From here back along the coast to Broadstairs the influence of and associations with Charles Dickens are all pervading. He lived both at Rochester and Broadstairs, and it was whilst he was living at Gad's Hill Place, Rochester, that Dickens was involved in a severe railway accident at Staplehurst on the Tonbridge to Ashford main line in June 1865. Scrambling from his derailed carriage he asked for his carriage key in order to release trapped passengers, for the practice of locking passengers into their compartments still persisted at this time. He came upon some fearful sights, 'the ruin of the carriages, the extraordinary weights under which the people were lying, or the complications into which they were twisted up among iron and wood, and mud and water'. He did what he could, giving brandy to a dying woman, helping a man to find his dead wife. He was terribly distressed and never completely recovered from the experience.

But let us leave the south with happier memories. Another immensely popular writer, Rudyard Kipling, had to move from his home on the LB&SCR near Brighton, because he was never able to get out of his front gate for autograph hunters, to Burwash, close to the SECR's Hastings line. He knew all about the boredom of the season ticket holder, but he also understood the excitement some of us feel whenever we set out on a train journey, to the country, to the seaside, to anywhere:

'Romance!' the season-tickets mourn,
'He never ran to catch his train,
But passed with coach and guard and horn
And left the local—late again!'

Confound Romance! . . . And all unseen
Romance brought up the nine-fifteen.

Across the Thames from the Isle of Sheppey is Canvey Island which developed as a holiday centre in the mid-nineteenth century and was meant to be served by a monorail. But it never was, and instead settled for acres of more or less static caravans, so we will move back out along the north shore of the Thames Estuary to Brighton's rival claimant to the title 'London by the Sea', Southend.

A 'Jaffa cake'-liveried 4CEP at Broadstairs, May 1989.

EAST ANGLIA

Southend-on-Sea

For those not brought up in London it may come as a surprise to realize the barrier which the Thames creates between north and south. On the whole, and for no clear logical reason which I can fathom, if one lives south of the river one tends to go on living on that side however much one may move around, and the converse is true for those on the north side. Similarly for those south of the river a day at the seaside usually means a Kent or Sussex resort whilst those on the north bank head for Essex or Suffolk.

Southend was the exception. For generations, since the second decade of the nineteenth century, a favourite day trip of Londoners had been to sail from Tower Pier or Greenwich down the river to Southend-on-Sea. There they disembarked at the longest pier in the world, a statistic which alone made the trip worthwhile, and rode all the way down it in a rattling electric toast-rack to the beach and the Kursaal amusements. My family was no exception. Long before I was born my grandfather and father had been regulars, and when the General Steam Navigation Company's paddle steamer *Royal Eagle* resumed her sailings after the war in 1946 I made the first of my many trips down what was still in those days the busiest waterway in the world. Dark red-sailed Thames barges were almost as common as the strings of lighters being towed up and down by steam

A Southend-bound EMU hurries past Leigh-on-Sea, December 1987.

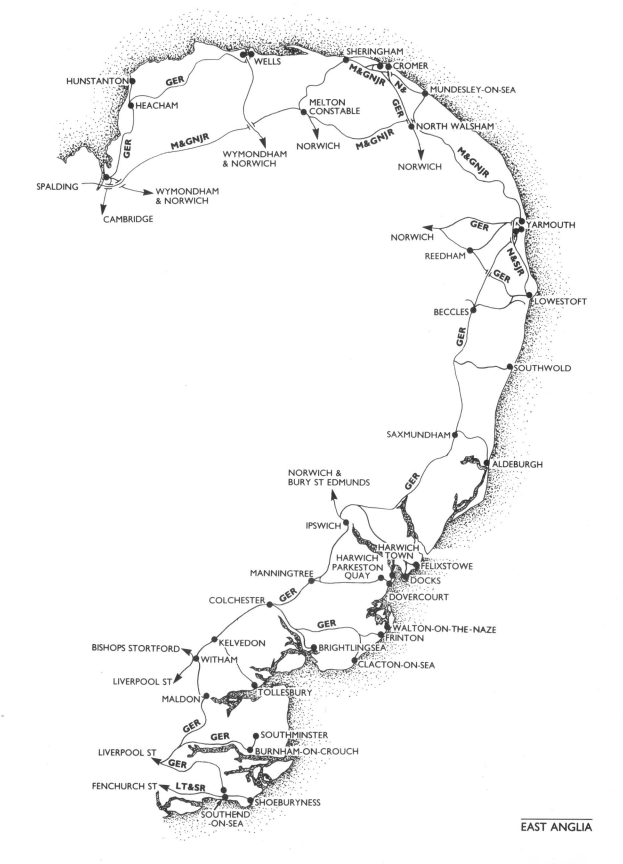

HUNSTANTON

HEACHAM

SPALDING

CAMBRIDGE

GER

GER

M&GNJR

WELLS

SHERINGHAM

CROMER

M&GNJR

N&

MUNDESLEY-ON-SEA

MELTON CONSTABLE

GER

NORWICH

M&GNJR

NORTH WALSHAM

WYMONDHAM & NORWICH

WYMONDHAM & NORWICH

M&GNJR

NORWICH

M&GNJR

NORWICH

GER

YARMOUTH

REEDHAM

N&SJR

GER

LOWESTOFT

BECCLES

GER

SOUTHWOLD

SAXMUNDHAM

ALDEBURGH

NORWICH & BURY ST EDMUNDS

GER

IPSWICH

HARWICH TOWN

HARWICH PARKESTON QUAY

FELIXSTOWE

MANNINGTREE

DOCKS

GER

DOVERCOURT

COLCHESTER

GER

WALTON-ON-THE-NAZE

FRINTON

BISHOPS STORTFORD

KELVEDON

BRIGHTLINGSEA

LIVERPOOL ST

WITHAM

CLACTON-ON-SEA

MALDON

TOLLESBURY

GER

GER

SOUTHMINSTER

LIVERPOOL ST

BURNHAM-ON-CROUCH

GER

FENCHURCH ST

LT&SR

SHOEBURYNESS

SOUTHEND -ON-SEA

EAST ANGLIA

and diesel tugs, whilst every type of steam and motor ship from ancient, tall-funnelled coasters and tramps to great white-hulled P&O liners provided an endless panorama which could not fail to fascinate even the most earthbound landlubber. I knew, of course, that it was also possible to get to Southend by train, behind 4–4–2Ts and 2–6–4Ts hauling long rakes of LMS-built non-corridor carriages, but the railway could hardly compete with the glamour of the steamers.

Although my initial view of Southend was of a cheap and cheerful, winkles and brown ale resort, devoted to catering for the needs of working class day-trippers from London intent on getting the last ha'pence of value for their hard-earned cash, there is another aspect to the town, one of considerable elegance and culture, epitomized by the Royal Terrace and other late eighteenth and early nineteenth century villas and squares in Clifftown, immediately west of the pier. For it was royalty, Princess Charlotte of Wales, who brought Southend fame at about the same time that the Prince Regent was completing his Royal Pavilion at Brighton.

Later, at the Assembly Rooms in the Royal Terrace, the initial meetings of the pier and the railway companies were held. When the bill for construction of the pier was passed in

Plaistow shed, London, Tilbury & Southend Railway, with a variety of 4–4–2Ts awaiting their next turns of duty in about 1914. (*Locomotive Publishing Co*)

1829, Southend was a distinctly superior, quiet seaside town of 2,462 souls. It took a long, long time until the pier was finished — not until 1891 — but meanwhile, in March 1856, the London, Tilbury & Southend Railway had arrived. Thirty-three years later, the Great Eastern Railway opened a terminus in the town centre at Victoria station at the end of its line from Liverpool Street. By 1892 the population had risen to 12,000. But this was as nothing for, with the two railway companies and the steamers competing with every weapon at their disposal, visitors to and would-be residents of the nearest seaside resort to the capital of the British Empire poured in, and by 1914 the County Borough of Southend-on-Sea had absorbed the nearby communities of Leigh-on-Sea, Southchurch, Prittlewell, Shoeburyness and others, and its population stood at 75,000.

The London, Tilbury & Southend Railway was taken over by the Midland in 1914, but its long tradition of building 4–4–2Ts to handle practically all its passenger traffic was continued, the last appearing under the LMS in 1930. The LT&SR also had some 4–6–4Ts,

which seemed to have a peculiar affinity with seaside lines — the Furness, Glasgow & South Western, County Down and London, Brighton & South Coast are examples that immediately spring to mind. The LT&SR 4–6–4Ts, which did not appear until Midland days, proved too heavy to work into Fenchurch Street, which although used by the company as its London terminus was actually owned by the GER, so they were banished to double-heading coal trains into Cricklewood, ending their days, like so many 'Baltic' tanks, prematurely and ignominiously. Stanier designed some three-cylinder 2–6–4Ts for the Tilbury and Southend line and the first of these, No 2500 is preserved, together with Tilbury 4–4–2T No 80 *Thundersley* of 1909, at Bressingham.

Southend's character has changed greatly in the last 30 years. Few families spend a holiday there and although it still attracts daytrippers these are but a pale shadow of the almost countless numbers which arrived by boat, train and charabanc in its heyday, which lasted until the 1950s.

Electrification came to the former LT&SR route in 1961, by which time it had become, logically, part of the Eastern Region. The rival route had been electrified at the beginning of 1957, doing away with the Great

Above The Pier tramway, Southend, December 1987.

Below Leigh-on-Sea, with a Fenchurch Street to Shoeburyness train approaching, December 1987.

Eastern inside-cylinder 4–6–0s which had worked it for so long, together with the more modern LNER 4–6–0s and other classes. However, the electric railway fell into disuse and the pier itself was at one time threatened, but the 1980s have seen a revival of both pier and trains, the latter now being diesel-powered. Locomotive-hauled excursions continued to appear, though in ever decreasing numbers.

The Fenchurch Street line continues on through Southend Central to Shoeburyness, long a naval and military area of importance guarding the entrance to the Thames Estuary. The simple, two-platform-plus-bay station with its unprepossessing wooden waiting room and booking office, is almost at the water's edge. Trains approach the station past a vast depot which houses the huge number of electric trains which are required, especially at peak times, to work this busy line.

There is an equally good service in and out of Southend's other principal station, Victoria. Both Central and Victoria stations, without being outstanding examples of railway architecture, have been quite successfully modernized whilst retaining a good deal of their pre-Grouping character. The Central route provides the best view of the sea — or the Thames, for it is not easy to determine where one ends and the other begins — running alongside it for several miles between Leigh-on-Sea and the approach to the town centre. The Victoria line is a totally inland route, which approaches the town past the airport and the sprawling northern suburbs.

Essex and Suffolk

The flat marshes of East Anglia may not have the instant appeal of the cliffs and sands of Devon and Cornwall or the dramatic hills sweeping down to the Clyde, but they have their own subtle quality. They are also a favourite haunt of yachtsmen, and Burnham-on-Crouch is one such town. A single track branch from the Great Eastern's Southend line reached it in 1889 and almost immediately killed off the coastal shipping trade. Still single track but now electrified, it serves what is apparently sometimes known as the 'Cowes of the East Coast' on account of its popularity with the sailing fraternity. Burnham is not quite the end of the branch for it turns inland and continues to Southminster and the Bradwell nuclear power station, which provides business for the railway.

There was a branch which left that to Burnham-on-Crouch at Woodham Ferrers, and headed north-east to Maldon, at the head of Blackwater estuary. Here it met another branch coming south-east from the Liverpool Street to Ipswich main line at Witham. Developers intended to build up Maldon as a harbour for agricultural products, but they went broke before the project got properly under way and although, once the railway arrived in 1848, the town saw some day-trippers, these never amounted to much. All trains ceased to run in 1964.

Further round the Blackwater estuary is the village of Tollesbury, which was endowed with a pier 1,770 feet long and had aspirations towards becoming a yachting centre. A light railway was opened from the main line at Kelvedon in 1904 by the GER, but neither the yachtsmen nor the holidaymakers turned up to travel upon it. The service, inevitably a sparse one, was however provided by some interesting, very non-standard tramway-type carriages in the charge of an 0–6–0T, but came to an end in 1951.

Brightlingsea sounds like a name thought up for a television situation comedy, but it is real enough and for a while nurtured ambitions to outshine nearby Clacton. Its branch was opened in 1866 and although, like many small East Coast ports close to the Thames estuary, the railway killed its commercial traffic, the yachts began to appear, as did day-trippers in modest numbers, until the line closed in 1964.

Clacton is in a sense the archetypal British seaside resort, for it was virtually created by the railway and grew from very little to a considerable amount as a consequence. When the

Great Eastern Railway arrived there in 1882 the population was just over 1,200, and even that was quite a bit more than it had been at the beginning of the century. A development plan was published for the resort at around this time, one that was followed quite closely with the result that by the turn of the century the population was 7,456 and it had become one of the most popular watering places in the country, not least because it was within easy reach of London, 70 miles from Liverpool Street.

Clacton is, or was, in a sense a counter-balance to Southend — very popular with Londoners, but approaching life at a rather more dignified pace. It is a neat, clean town, with spacious, flat, tree-lined avenues, a functional concrete pier, no beach to speak of at high tide, the heaviest tea trays in the British Isles, two theatres, and an air of never quite having got beyond 1936. This did not prevent British Railways from electrifying the Clacton line ready for the 1959 summer season, although, curiously, it was not until 1962 that the entire route to London was electrified and the Class '309' express multiple units entered service. With their wrap-around driving cab windows they had pretentions to style lacking in their Southern Region contemporaries, and indeed were the first British express electric units not intended for Southern service.

Walton-on-the-Naze and Clacton stations both see substantial commuter traffic, to London and to Colchester and Chelmsford. The Walton branch was electrified at the same time as that to Clacton; its penultimate station is Frinton-on-Sea, and like Clacton both resorts really owe their existence to the Great Eastern Railway, although neither was ever a serious rival to the larger resort. Frinton, in particular, would have shuddered at such a notion, taking pride in claiming to be the most sedate resort in the country and the only one which has not a single public house. There are those amongst its residents who considered that the opening of its station was an invitation to the devil to take up residence, an opportunity of which he does not yet seem to have availed himself.

Harwich and Felixstowe, twin ports on opposite sides of the River Orwell, have in recent years taken full advantage of their East Coast proximity to the great European ports clustered around the Rhine estuary, and since the advent of the Common market have increased their trade, outstripping many west coast ports now in decline. Although Harwich, with its relatively deep water, had been a port for centuries before the railway came, it was still a very small, though quite important, town when its branch line arrived in 1854. By then it looked as if it had lost out to Ipswich, which, possessing a railway station and extensive rail-served docks as early as 1846, had taken over as the port for the Dutch steamers.

Class '302' EMUs at Harwich, February 1989.

Clacton station in August 1987.

However, the Great Eastern Railway decided that Harwich did have a future and between 1879 and 1883 spent over £1½ million on reclaiming land west of the original port. It named this new port Parkeston after its chairman, but although the name persists to this day and its station is officially entitled Harwich Parkeston Quay, as far as the locals are concerned it is all part of Harwich. Between Parkeston Quay and Harwich Town stations (the end of the line) is Dovercourt. Until fairly recently it carried the suffix 'Bay', and there has been a small resort here with a sandy beach for over 200 years. Today the station is the principal one for the town of Harwich.

The Harwich branch leaves the main line by a triangular junction at Manningtree, the latter claiming to be the windiest station in the British Isles. Trains on the main line slow to 25 mph to cross the viaduct over the River Stour, which joins the Orwell at Harwich, and from the viaduct one can look down the wide Stour to the ships off Harwich and Felixstowe. The branch remains within sight of the Stour for all of its 11½ miles. It is an attractive stretch of railway and there is a distinctively Scandinavian feel about this part of East Anglia. There are some very fine and rather remarkable wooden buildings, mills,

storehouses and homes around Ipswich and at various places on or near the coast, most of the carriages on the main-line trains carry notices in English, Dutch, German and Swedish, there are many travellers and a vast amount of freight coming from or heading to northern Europe through Ipswich, Felixstowe and Harwich, and there are trees stretching down to the water's edge.

The first station on the Harwich branch, Mistley, is quite dwarfed by a tall brick chimney embossed with the legend 'Malt Extract Works' towering high above it. There is a siding which leads down to the quay, although it is rusty and overgrown. Next comes Wrabness, a distinctive little wayside station with the body of an old GER five-compartment, six-wheel carriage adjoining the brick station house set in front of an expanse of grass leading to the platform edge. The electric trains speed on with views across the meadows, where horses graze, stretching to the greeny brown mud and the water beyond, before the trees take over again, although it is still possible to see through the topmost branches the water and ships at anchor.

Harwich is coming up fast now and the

The Hook of Holland boat train at Liverpool Street in September 1980, with two 1960-built Metro-Cammell Pullmans prominent.

train heads back towards the water's edge, weaving its way through extensive sidings with perhaps one of the big Scandinavian or Hook of Holland ferries, as large as a fair-sized liner, tied up beside the handsome red brick terminal. For a long time Harwich depended solely on the railway and although this is no longer so, proportionally the railborne traffic is vastly greater than at almost any other port in the British Isles with a constant succession of liner trains pulling out and heading either through Ipswich and on to the Midlands and the North or through Colchester to London and the south.

The Great Eastern and later the LNE railways took considerable pride in their Continental expresses, which were monopolized for the first half of this century by 4-6-0s, first the Great Eastern '1500' inside-cylinder class, and then by the Gresley three-cylinder 'B17s' and the Thompson two-cylinder 'B1s'. In January 1900, *The Railway Magazine* featured the Parkeston to York express in its 'World-Famous Trains' series, which must have surprised a few people as one would hardly have put it in the same class as the

'Flying Scotsman', the 'Blue Train' or the 'Trans-Siberian Express'. The magazine did admit that 'There are doubtless more famous trains in England than this cross country one' but went on to claim that 'it is famous throughout the Continent . . . at Hamburg and Berlin, at Cologne and Basle, even as far as distant Vienna, its utility is known and appreciated'. The service originally only ran as far as Doncaster; a restaurant car was added in 1891. The GER had long harboured ambitions in a northerly direction, with the connivance of the North Eastern Railway. From 1 November 1892 the 'Continental' began to operate over the Cathedrals Route, by way of Ipswich, Bury St Edmunds (which although it doesn't actually possess a cathedral has a very distinguished parish church), Ely, Peterborough and Lincoln. Later it served Manchester and Liverpool.

Today there are no fewer than three evocatively named expresses over this route, the 'Loreley' to Birmingham, the 'North West Dane' to Blackpool, and the 'Rhinelander' to Manchester. 'Super Sprinters' have taken over from some of the first generation DMUs and are comfortable and speedy, their only drawback being shortage of accommodation if only two cars are employed. Some local services between

Ipswich and Harwich are worked by EMUs.

In 1924 the LNER inaugurated a train ferry service from Harwich to Hook of Holland, and although, unlike the rival Dover route, it never carried passenger vehicles, freight traffic boomed, much of it perishable dairy products. The revival after the Second World War was nothing short of dramatic, and the amount of the nation's goods passing through Harwich and Felixstowe had risen from 2.5 per cent in 1913 to 9.8 per cent in 1973. The two East Coast ports virtually equalled that of the combined total of Liverpool and Birkenhead, which 60 years earlier had been ten times greater. Containerization and Ro-Ro motor and rail traffic played a considerable part in this dramatic change-round.

The Felixstowe Railway and Pier Company was bought out by private enterprise in 1951 and when the new container ports were opened here and at Harwich in 1968, taking advantage of deep water, the lack of traditional work practices and good communications, both road and rail (a new line into the docks was opened as recently as the 1980s), with the Midlands, the boom really got under way. However, Felixstowe is not only a commercial port, but also has a beach and a handsome station dating from 1898 a few minutes walk away from the water. Nowadays a single platform suffices and little of the station building is actually in railway use any more, most of it having been converted into a shopping centre.

The Harwich line was electrified in 1986 and the frequency of the service improved, but the Ipswich to Felixstowe branch, which is single track, remains diesel operated. DMUs have a monopoly of the passenger traffic, and although none work beyond Ipswich, the new electrified service on the main line means that it is possible to reach Felixstowe from Liverpool Street in less than two hours.

Aldeburgh will forever be associated with Benjamin Britten and the music festival he founded and which is now the largest in the country. Sadly, no one comes to Aldeburgh by train any more, unless they alight at Sax-mundham on the Ipswich to Lowestoft line, and thence take a taxi or bus. The Aldeburgh branch was opened from Saxmundham in 1860 and gave a great boost to the herring and sprat fishing fleets, although the gradual silting up of the harbour spelt their eventual doom. Visitors also came to Aldeburgh, although the station was half a mile from the sea. It lasted until Dr Beeching decided it was no longer needed and closed the branch in 1966, all except for a section which serves the controversial nuclear power station at Sizewell, situated between the branch's two intermediate stations at Leiston and Thorpeness.

Southwold is an attractive little resort, midway between Aldeburgh and Lowestoft, but the Great Eastern Railway, after some deliberation decided it would never generate sufficient revenue to make a branch line worthwhile. However, Southwold was determined to be put on the railway map and in 1879 the only narrow gauge line in East Anglia, the 3-foot Southwold Railway, opened. It might have been the precursor of the 'Titfield Thunderbolt', so curious, antiquated and slow were its services, and, to quote H.C. Casserley, 'by 1929 its ancient rolling stock could no longer withstand the all-conquering bus competition', and it gave up the ghost.

Lowestoft and Yarmouth

East Anglia may not be a particularly heavily populated area of Great Britain but this did not prevent it being served by a dense network of railways. Less surprisingly, both before and during the Beeching years a ferocious cutback saw many Norfolk and Suffolk branch lines disappear, and what was claimed to be the first main-line closure in England take place. During the 1950s and '60s, rural East Anglia possessed a greater number of cars in relation to the size of the population than anywhere else in Britain, so it is not perhaps surprising that traffic on the railways declined. A typical East Anglian branch line train of a couple of ancient,

'Britannia' 'Pacific' No. 70030 *William Wordsworth*
passing Stratford with the 1 pm from Great Yarmouth,
4 June 1960.

wooden-bodied carriages hauled by a Great
Eastern 0-6-0 or 2-4-0 meandering beneath
the scudding white clouds and deep blue skies
which have inspired generations of painters
may have pleased the lovers of the picturesque; prospective passengers with somewhere
to get to in a hurry merely took to their cars.

A Victorian guidebook described Lowestoft
as the 'Most easterly point of England, upon
a lofty eminence, rising abruptly from the
German Sea'. The town and its fierce rival
Great Yarmouth vigorously promoted rail
links, not simply — perhaps not even
primarily — to encourage holiday trade but
to outdo each other in the shipping and
fishing industries. In the early years of the
last century, Norwich was still a busy port
reached by river both by way of Great Yarmouth and Lowestoft. The latter settled the
issue when the Norwich & Lowestoft Navigation Company was created in 1827 to build a
canal. In 1833, the year the canal opened,

some 200 vessels sailed along it into Norwich.
However, its success was short-lived. Ships
were getting bigger, too big to reach inland
ports such as Norwich, but much more im- ·
portantly the railway could carry people, mer-
chandise and fish infinitely faster. New
markets were opening up and with the construction of Britain's most easterly station at
Lowestoft in 1847, at the end of an 11½-mile
branch from Reedham on the Norwich to
Great Yarmouth line, and its adjoining fish
dock, fish could now be sent as far as Manchester guaranteed fresh on arrival. Great
Yarmouth was equally quick to seize the new
opportunities and the huge fishing fleets of the
two ports became dependent upon the Great
Eastern Railway to speed their catches to the
markets of London, the Midlands and the
North. Samuel Peto, the builder of Yarmouth's first railway, bought the Norwich &
Lowestoft Navigation Company in 1844, and
18 years later the GER bought the harbour at
Lowestoft and did all it could to encourage
the fish business, constructing a new dock.

The holiday trade was expanding with
equal vigour. Great Yarmouth had its sea

Holiday crowds at Great Yarmouth, August 1987.

baths, assembly rooms, library and theatre by 1800 and Lowestoft had introduced bathing machines in 1768. With the coming of the railway, the population of Lowestoft doubled in 16 years to around 10,000 and had reached 36,000 by the end of the century. In 1849 Peto constructed the esplanade, the same year that the Royal Hotel opened. Despite its great expansion, Lowestoft always remained a good deal smaller than its rival up the coast and preferred it that way. Quieter and rather more refined, a visitor in 1880 described Lowestoft as the 'cleanest, neatest and most orderly seaside spot'.

Great Yarmouth, however, developed considerable pretensions to grandeur and the Victoria Building Company set about attempting to rival the elegance of Brighton. But it wasn't what the customers wanted. Almost all of the visitors came by train (although some came on the daily boat from London), and in the first year of the August Bank Holiday 82,559 visitors arrived in Great Yarmouth, around double the population of the town. They came principally from the East End of London and the industrial cities of the Midlands and Yorkshire and were interested, not in elegance and studied leisure, but in getting the greatest return on the money they had spent on their precious week beside the

sea. The beach, a bathe in the sea, an inexpensive boarding house, sideshows and a 'veritable line of music hall minstrelsy' were what was required and Great Yarmouth made sure there was plenty of all of it.

Dickens liked Great Yarmouth town, possibly because it reminded him of Brighton, which he knew well, for it had been a fashionable resort from the end of the eighteenth century, following in Brighton's footsteps. He would have travelled to Yarmouth by train, a line having been opened on 1 May 1844 to Norwich, the latter being linked to London just over a year later when the route through Cambridge, Ely and Thetford came into use. The Norwich-Great Yarmouth line was surveyed by the Stephensons, father and son, George and Robert, and Peto was the resident engineer, employing some 1,500 men. The importance of Great Yarmouth may be judged by the fact that its line to Norwich was the very first in Norfolk. Eventually the town would boast three terminus stations, the original Vauxhall, then South Town in 1859 and finally Beach in 1877.

South Town station was originally owned by the East Suffolk Railway, but was worked, like Vauxhall, from the outset by the Eastern Counties. The line to South Town originated at Ipswich, and passed through Wickham Market and Beccles. This became the recognized route for London to Great Yar-

mouth expresses. The third station, Beach, belonged to neither the Eastern Counties nor the Great Eastern, and only became LNER property in 1936. It was served by the Midland & Great Northern Railway.

This was a joint line which served much of the Norfolk coast and which has all but vanished today. It was an amalgam of all sorts of obscure little lines and assumed the title by which it is remembered in the summer of 1893. A good many local people also knew it as the Muddle and Get Nowhere, which was apt if rather unkind. It did the best it could, extending in a wiggly arc from Saxby, on the Midland Railway's Melton Mowbray to Kettering branch, and from the Great Northern main line at Peterborough. The two sections linked up at Sutton Bridge (one of several junctions of that name — this one was just below the Wash) to form the main line, albeit single track, which continued on to the M&GN headquarters at Melton Constable. There one line headed up to the coastal resorts of Sheringham and Cromer, a second turned south-east for Norwich, whilst a third continued eastwards into Broads country and the coast immediately north of Great

Yarmouth. The route was slow and single-tracked for virtually its entire length but it carried its share of visitors from the Midlands, although the majority used the Great Eastern line through Ely and Norwich.

Late Victorian Great Yarmouth was popular and prosperous. It acquired a tramway as early as 1875 which, as befitted a forward-looking municipality, was electrified early in the present century. In equally progressive manner, buses replaced the trams in 1933. The Great Eastern Railway served the town well and by 1904 was running non-stop expresses to and from Liverpool Street, hauled by the excellent 'Claud Hamilton' 4-4-0s in 150 minutes. This was quite splendid and was not to be surpassed, not even during the high speed era of the 1930s. In 1987 the fastest runs occupied 15 minutes longer, although there can be no direct comparison for these included no fewer than seven stops, a longer distance and reversal at Norwich.

In the 1930s, following the success of the

'B17' No 61664 *Liverpool* at Bentley Gates with the 18.34 Yarmouth South Town–Ipswich, August 1957. (*Colour-Rail*)

East Coast streamliners, the LNER introduc-ed the 'East Anglian' express between Nor-wich and Liverpool Street and streamlined two 'B17' 4–6–0s to haul it. The 'Hook Con-tinental' was also fitted out with a set of brand new carriages and these were rather more distinctive than the 'East Anglian', be-ing of open layout throughout and very similar to the high-speed 'Coronation' sets. Unusually for a 1930s named train, the 'Hook Continental' set resumed work in 1945 and indeed continued to serve Parkeston Quay boat passengers until 1963–4. Earlier, in 1928, Gresley had introduced his three-cylinder 'B17' Class 4–6–0s very much with the former Great Eastern main line, and the Harwich boat train and Southend services in particular, in mind. They performed well enough but could never match the best that the LMS and GWR big express 4–6–0s regularly achieved, and it is significant that they never really replaced the Great Eastern 4–6–0s, many of which were rebuilt by Gresley. When Thompson brought out his two-cylinder 'B1' 4–6–0s during the Second World War they took over much of the 'B17's' top link work, despite being rough-riding, mixed traffic engines. It wasn't until 1951, with the introduction of the first batch of the first British Railways standard design, the 'Britannia' 'Pacifics', that the Norwich, and later the Great Yarmouth, Lowestoft, Clacton and King's Lynn express services, received really top class motive power.

The 'Britannia' reign lasted less than ten years, for dieselization came early to East Anglia and by 21 March 1960 just under half of the passenger and just over half of the freight services were being worked by diesel traction, and nearly half of the entire British Railways main-line diesel fleet was concen-trated here. Ipswich depot was the first to become completely dieselized, whilst Norwich and Stratford (the largest in the country), which were the main suppliers of motive power for many of the coast lines, both branch and main, soon followed suit.

With the 1950s came the inevitable decline in the railway scene at Great Yarmouth. The Midland & Great Northern's Beach station closed in 1959, and 11 years later Yarmouth South Town went. This left the town served by two lines, both from Norwich, one via Reedham, the other via Acle. Fishing had been in decline for years and with the transfer of what was left of this trade to the roads, the extensive network of lines serving the docks and quays, worked by tram engines, their wheels and motion enclosed like Victorian matrons, was abandoned. Each station had once had its own engine shed, but with the advent of diesels these too became redundant.

Great Yarmouth's remaining station, Vauxhall, has no architectural merit and is not very convenient for passengers or staff, but it does plenty of business and, unlike many seaside termini, still handles much holi-day traffic in the summer months.

On the main line, diesel power was to be only an interim stage. The special train which

inaugurated the full electric service between Liverpool Street and Norwich on 11 May 1987 did the return journey in 83 minutes 22 seconds, reaching a maximum speed of 107 mph, quite putting all previous records in the shade. It would be possible for a direct service between Great Yarmouth and London to easily beat the old 150-minute record, despite having to travel via Norwich since the closing of the direct South Town-Haddiscoe-Beccles line, but there does not seem to be the demand for a non-stop service today. At least there are still through trains, and not just to London. On weekdays there is a restaurant car train from Liverpool Lime Street to Great Yarmouth, and on summer Saturdays trains from Birmingham, Newcastle and Leeds.

In contrast, Lowestoft station is very nearly the best place in town to get away from the holiday crowds. On summer Saturdays it is served by ten trains from Ipswich and 18 from Norwich, all DMUs. Long-distance trains were always rather more scarce at Lowestoft than at Great Yarmouth, although the town once had a regular Liverpool Street service, but now there are none. The station itself, set beside the docks and very close to the front, is not without distinction. It is built of yellowish grey brick, like so many in Eastern England, and reminds one instantly of parts of King's Cross and Liverpool Street. There was still a large Eastern Region royal blue enamel sign on its façade in the summer of 1987, and with its varnished wood bookstall, plethora of supports for the twin spans of its overall roof, and battery of semaphore signals it has a very 1950s, or even earlier, atmosphere. There were even three old LNER teak-bodied carriages in the sidings in departmental use and the remains of a Gresley tender to strengthen the illusion.

Unlike Great Yarmouth, Lowestoft retains its goods yard, which is right beside the docks. These latter, as at Great Yarmouth, still accommodate a fair-sized fishing fleet, but much newer, although already part of a tradition, are the sturdy-looking supply boats which service the oil rigs out in the North Sea.

There was once a direct line between Great Yarmouth and Lowestoft, rejoicing in the lengthy title, The Norfolk & Suffolk Joint Railways Committee, owned by the Great Eastern Railway and the Midland & Great Northern Joint Railway. It lasted until 1970 and served the resort of Gorleston, im-

mediately south of Yarmouth. Indeed, it served it so well that it provided it with no fewer than three Gorleston stations, Golf Links, Gorleston-on-Sea and Gorleston North. There was, and indeed is, an alternative rail link between the two resorts. A 20-minute run on the Lowestoft-Norwich line brings one to Reedham, and by changing there on to a Norwich-Great Yarmouth train, with a wait of sometimes no more than five minutes, one can complete the journey in 45 minutes. From town centre to town centre this is often as good as the time by car, and sometimes considerably better.

Haddiscoe, the station before Reedham on the line out of Lowestoft, was once an important junction where the Beccles to Yarmouth line crossed it; one of its signal boxes has staked a claim to immortality for it has been reassembled in the Science Museum at South Kensington and is there for all to see as the

representative of the many thousands of manual signal boxes, for so long a feature of every stretch of railway line in the British Isles, but now fast vanishing. It should be said, however, that there are still a good few in East Anglia, Lowestoft and Great Yarmouth each possessing handsome versions of the standard GER box.

First station out of Yarmouth Beach on the M&GN Joint line was Caister Beach. Next was Caister Camp Halt, and this brings us to one of the most significant developments in the story of holidays by the sea, one in which the railway played a significant part.

Holiday camps and poppies

In 1906 a philanthropist, Fletcher Dodd, organized a summer camp for Socialist families from the East End of London amongst the dunes immediately behind the beach at Caister-on-Sea. For many it was

East Anglian holiday. Great Eastern-built 'D16/3' 4–4–0 No 62511 in charge of the 10.15 Liverpool Street to Gorleston just beats a cyclist to the bridge at Hopton-on-Sea, June 1957. (*E. Alger/Colour-Rail*)

their first holiday and their first experience of the sea, and so popular was it that the camp was repeated the following year. In a short time it developed into a commercial enterprise with wooden chalets replacing the original tents. Resuming after the First World War, it attracted yet more customers, Entertainment halls were built and for two guineas one got accommodation, food for the week and travel to and from Great Yarmouth station.

One of the reasons for the phenomenal success of the enterprise was its high standards and strict rules. Each camper had to wear a badge so that he or she could be identified and interlopers banished, everyone had to be safely within the gates at 11 pm and there was no gambling, drinking of alcohol or children under the age of two. A brochure for 1924 advertises that the 'camp stands on high ground and can be approached by train, tram or bus'. The Midland & Great Northern Joint opened a station right beside the camp, but the majority of passengers would have come to either Great Yarmouth Vauxhall or South Town stations and thence by special bus.

Thus it was that holiday camps originated. Once the success of Caister camp was established, others began to be set up, along the Norfolk and Suffolk coast and all over Britain. The original has long since disappeared, but there are still holiday camps at Caister, Great Yarmouth and Lowestoft and buses still meet the trains at Great Yarmouth to collect the jolly campers.

A series of halts followed in close succession after Caister including the exotically named California, before the line turned in a little from the sea and negotiated its way through the Broads. Potter Heigham is a great boating centre and the M&GN provided two stations, a halt at the bridge and another in the centre of the village. Nowadays much of the route has become the Weaver's Way, a path for walkers which takes its name from the weavers who would walk that part of the world in Medieval times with wool from the tens of thousands of sheep which grazed the fields bordering the streams, the rivers, and the lakes.

Elsewhere the A149 follows the trackbed of the railway. At North Walsham it met the Great Eastern's still extant Norwich to Cromer line, and the branch to Mundesley-on-Sea. This latter, like the line between Yarmouth and Lowestoft, rejoiced in the complication of being jointly owned by a joint company and one other, ie the M&GNJR and the GER. The branch was opened in July 1898 and nine years later was extended along the coast to Cromer.

Mundesley has a stout wall to keep back the sea, the village (or is it a town?) lies behind the low, grassy cliffs. Through carriages ran between Mundesley-on-Sea and Liverpool Street, but traffic was always light and by the 1920s conductor-guards were put in charge of selling tickets, Mundesley being the only station of the six between North Walsham and Cromer which issued them. The line to Cromer closed in 1953, the North Walsham line and consequently Mundesley station going 11 years later.

Cromer has fared better. One of its two stations has gone but it retains the other, and on it is a sign proclaiming that Cromer is 'The Gem of the Norfolk Coast'. It is indeed a pleasant, dignified town, set upon the cliffs which face the North Sea.

The first line to reach Cromer was that of the Great Eastern from Norwich which opened in March 1877. Immediately the town began to expand and a number of hotels date from the last two decades of the nineteenth century. Ten years later, the Eastern & Midlands Railway arrived from King's Lynn and Melton Constable. This would eventually become the Midland & Great Northern Joint, but the initials E&MR can still be seen in the ironwork of the station buildings, as can those of the M&GNR. These buildings, in mock Tudor style, now belong to a builders' merchants which has also taken over the goods yard. The station itself, Cromer Beach as it used to be to distinguish it from the now vanished Great Eastern's High, consists of an island platform with a modern, neat little brick waiting room, the original signal box and semaphore signals. Above the buffer stops is a red-painted oil lamp embossed with the initials 'LNE (GE SECT)'. The station isn't quite as near the beach as its title would suggest, but it's handy enough, a brisk seven or eight minutes' walk away.

Cromer High closed in 1954, but it was a loss which could be borne for it was rather inconveniently placed high above the town and its trains were diverted to the more accessible Beach station. Cromer has played host to much holiday traffic over the years, the most distinguished being the 'Eastern Belle', the all-Pullman holiday train which the LNER ran between the wars.

The line from Norwich passes through pretty countryside which has come to be known as Poppyland; the writer and critic Clement Scott, who was extremely fond of the area, bestowed the name on it around the turn of the century. Beyond Cromer the DMUs continue along the coast to their destination at Sheringham, four miles distant. The GER is left behind and we are now in M&GN territory. However, the station which serves as the terminus of the branch is a BR construction, but one of its least distinguished architectural efforts, being a mere collection of asphalt-covered sleepers. Immediately across the road which leads down through the centre of Sheringham to the beach is the real station. This belongs to the North Norfolk Railway, the present-day successor of the old Midland & Great Northern Joint.

Varnished teak

The Midland & Great Northern had much in common with that other well-known line, the Somerset & Dorset, not least its precarious prospects. Both concerns possessed single-track main lines which sidled their way across not very populous parts of England. They served their customers to the best of their limited abilities in a friendly and courteous manner and were liked for it.

Midland & Great Northern engines were painted in a striking yellow livery. It may not have been as celebrated as the Brighton's 'improved engine green' but it lasted a lot longer, down to 1929 when, as on the Brighton, it was replaced by a more sombre brown. Carriages were varnished teak, and in later years these were a fascinating collection of antiquities, obtained at knockdown prices from the LMS and LNER, being of various pre-Grouping origins.

The Melton Constable to Sheringham line outlived almost all the rest of the M&GN system and did not succumb until 1964. By this date a preservation society had been formed and out of this the present North Norfolk Railway grew. The original M&GN engines had all long gone by then, as had the carriages, but a Great Eastern-built 'J15 0-6-0, No, 564, a type once common throughout East Anglia, is regularly in steam today. 'B12' No, 1572, the sole surviving former GER 4-6-0, another type native to these parts, is completing a lengthy restoration at Weybourne.

There were still some LNER carriages around in 1964 which had once worn the distinctive varnished teak livery, and some found their way into preservation on the North Norfolk Railway. A particularly interesting group is the four-coach articulated set built for suburban services out of King's Cross in 1924, but quite the most splendid is the beautifully restored Gresley buffet car No 51769. The team largely responsible for what is probably the most authentic former LNER carriage still in existence consisted of just two people, Steve Allen, who became involved in the project in 1976 at the age of 16, and Dr Christine Ingram, wife of a volunteer driver on the North Norfolk Railway. There cannot be many Cambridge graduate lady radiologists in the preservation movement, and even fewer who have made all 28 curtains for a Gresley buffet car on their sitting room floor, to say nothing of reconstructing the bar. No 51769 can often be found sitting in No 2 platform at Sheringham, just as through carriages did after arrival from Liverpool Street in LNER days.

Sheringham is not unlike Cromer both in

character and in size and the two resorts have long been friendly — well, relatively friendly — rivals. Around the turn of the century, fast expresses connected both resorts with London. By 1896 the GER reached Cromer in three hours from Liverpool Street, whilst the GNR did its best to compete, using the metals of its ally the M&GN for the final $83\frac{1}{4}$ miles from Peterborough, with a schedule of $3\frac{3}{4}$ hours. Although a good deal slower than the GER route, the GNR trains also served Sheringham and thus provided real competition. In 1906 the connection between the GER and the M&GN lines at Cromer was put in and thus through trains could, and did, run direct to both resorts from Liverpool Street and from King's Cross.

British Rail continued to use Sheringham station after the line to Melton Constable had closed, but after the present collection of sleepers was dumped on the other side of the level crossing to form the new terminus, the proper station was handed over to the preservationists. This is now their headquarters and from it public steam trains once again began to run in July 1975. At present the line extends through Weybourne, a pleasant station, though a good distance from the seaside village it was built to serve, and on inland to Holt, $5\frac{1}{4}$ miles from Sheringham.

That really was the end of the M&GN's seaside connections, unless one counts King's Lynn, which is a port but neither a resort nor quite on the open sea. The rest of Norfolk, the north-east corner, belonged to the Great Eastern, and consisted of the Wells and the Hunstanton lines. Both have gone.

Wells-next-the-Sea was served by two lines, a branch from Wymondham on the Cambridge and Ely to Norwich line, through Dereham and Fakenham, and another from Heacham on the King's Lynn to Hunstanton line. To quote *The Railway Magazine* of May 1929, 'Wells was at one time a port of some importance but counts for little now'. The harbour's loss was the resort's gain, for it is now a large boating lake. But it is not a very big resort and could not support a train service beyond the Beeching years. Four to five trains a day were all that was thought necessary on both its branches, which were single track. The Heacham one, which opened in August 1866, closed in early BR days, in 1952, the other, dating from 1857, 11 years later in 1963.

What is believed to be the world's longest

'B12' 4–6–0 No 61572 undergoing restoration on the North Norfolk Railway in August 1987.

A Gresley LNER buffet car at Sheringham, formerly M&GNR but now the North Norfolk Railway.

10¼ inch gauge steam railway, the Wells & Walsingham Light Railway, now occupies four miles of the Wymondham to Wells track bed. It is the creation of one man, a retired naval commander, Roy Francis, and runs every day from Easter to the end of September. Motive power as I write is a handsome Garratt locomotive.

The Eastern Counties main line from Cambridge to King's Lynn was extended to Hunstanton in October 1862. One of Hunstanton's first day-trippers had been the much maligned King John who, passing by on his way from King's Lynn to Newark, decided to send his belongings, including much of the royal treasure, on a short cut across the Wash by way of the sands at Hunstanton, miscalculated the tide, and lost the lot.

Hunstanton is not very big — the population today is around 4,000 — but although the coming of the railway certainly boosted its popularity, it had been a favoured resort, in a small way, since the late eighteenth century. The Hunstanton branch was pretty high-class stuff, for not only was it constructed chiefly on account of the desire of the local lords of the manor, the L'Estrange family, to turn the town into a fully fledged resort, but nine months before it was opened the Royal Family bought the Sandringham estate; the nearby Wolferton station, midway between King's Lynn and Hunstanton, saw many celebrated visitors, notably Queen Victoria, and every British crowned head down to our present Queen. A special royal link was established at

King's Lynn shed and the locomotives which worked the Royal Trains were naturally hand-picked and kept in spotless condition. Great Eastern-built 'Claud Hamilton' 4-4-0s were much favoured, as was the 'B17' (later 'B2') Class 4-6-0 No. 1671 *Royal Sovereign*. Both King George V and King George VI died at Sandringham and the funeral trains conveyed their bodies from Wolferton. In the latter instance, No 70000 *Britannia* had charge of the train from King's Lynn.

The Hunstanton line was not merely a branch, for at the Grouping there were five through trains to and from Liverpool Street. In the late 1930s the fastest buffet car express took just over three hours for the 112 miles. This was not very fast, and through trains had to reverse in and out of King's Lynn, but the service was convenient and did good business. After the Second World War the most popular Liverpool Street train was named the 'Fenman'; there were also summer Saturday services to Birmingham and other Midland towns and cities. With the introduction of diesel multiple units in 1959, through services ceased and heavily laden holidaymakers had to change at King's Lynn. To BR's surprise they did not much like this and took to the road instead. The Hunstanton branch became a basic railway in 1966 with conductor-guards, unmanned level crossings, no freight services and the lifting of run-round facilities at Hunstanton. Despite not being listed for closure by Beeching, and despite great and justified local objections, the branch met its end in the spring of 1969.

THE EAST COAST

The Jolly Fisherman

We now move out of Great Eastern territory and into Great Northern. The long, flat Lincolnshire coast is relatively sparsely populated, particularly around the Wash. Boston was once the second busiest port in England, long, long ago, but when the railway arrived in 1884 it had greatly declined. Not beyond redemption, however, for even today its quays are still rail connected. The celebrated parish church, the Boston Stump, was built from the proceeds of the wool export business and the town boasts a splendid collection of dockside buildings of many periods. However, Boston is on an estuary and was never a resort.

The first one we come to is Skegness, yet another resort which owes its existence to the combined efforts of a noble lord — the Earl of Scarborough — and a railway company, and once through trains began to operate, its long, sandy beach soon attracted East Midlanders by the thousands.

Skegness will forever be associated with what is surely the most famous seaside poster of all time. John Hassall, a 40-year-old artist who had had pictures hung in the Royal Academy and drawings published in *Punch*, was commissioned by the Great Northern Railway in 1908 to design a poster for Skegness and he hit on the idea of featuring a jolly fisherman leaping along the sands above the slogan 'Skegness is so bracing', and below that the information that 'the cheapest and best half-day excursion from London non-stop corridor trains' left King's Cross at 11.30 am and cost 3s (15p). Hassall explained that his

Skegness's famous Jolly Fisherman strides across the station concourse and heads towards the beach for a breath of East Coast ozone — which was particularly bracing that October Saturday afternoon with a Force 9 whipping up the sand and the North Sea.

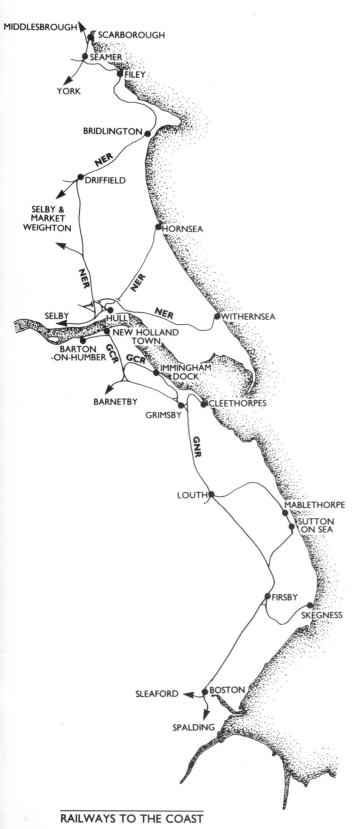

design 'had something to do with Romulus and Remus jumping over the little walls of Rome, and Skegness with its glorious air and sands making people jump without anything to jump over'. Which is as may be.

The jolly fisherman proved to be universally and irresistibly appealing. The GNR used him for the rest of its existence and when the LNER, those past masters of the seaside poster, took him over, they simplified and boldened him, added the newly erected pier and a dark red sailed boat, and so arrived at the classic British seaside poster. Hassall was paid £12 for his original design, but the real value was that it made him far more famous than any of his paintings had ever done. Skegness town council showed its deep gratitude for the fame the fat fisherman had brought them by incorporating him in the mayoral chain, erecting a statue of him, and sending an effigy of him in wreath form to John Hassall's funeral in 1948. Finally, to tie the story up neatly, or rather to give it a perfect beginning, we must record that Hassell was born beside the sea at Walmer in Kent.

Despite the GNR's advertising of cheap excursions from King's Cross — not surprising, for Skegness was virtually the only sizeable resort on which it held a monopoly — it has been from the East Midlands that most trippers and holidaymakers have over the years come to Skegness. The direct line from the south, from Peterborough, Spalding and Boston, closed in 1961, and the only approach now is from the west, from Sleaford, where the London, Lincoln, Nottingham and Sheffield lines come together, to Boston, then northwards to Firsby, where an abrupt swing to the east takes the line towards the coast and Skegness.

With a population of 12,500, the town was never in much danger of losing its railway, even during the Beeching years. Through trains operate from Crewe, Derby and Nottingham and on summer weekends well-patronized extras still bring holidaymakers by the thousand. A remote extension from the main BR network, the Skegness line is

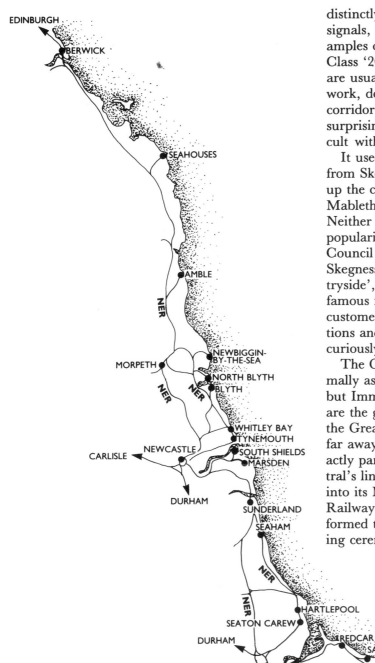

distinctly old-fashioned with its semaphore
signals, including, as I write, the last examples of the classic GNR somersault, and
Class '20' diesel-electric locomotives, which
are usually to be found exclusively on freight
work, double-heading rakes of elderly Mark 1
corridor trains at a leisurely pace. It is not
surprising that it has become something of a
cult with enthusiasts of late.

It used to be possible to travel by train
from Skegness to Firsby and then northwards
up the coast to Sutton-on-Sea and
Mablethorpe, but this branch closed in 1970.
Neither resort ever approached the size or
popularity of Skegness. East Lindsey District
Council currently advertises Mablethorpe and
Skegness together as 'The seaside in the countryside', not forgetting to include Hassall's
famous fisherman, and invites prospective
customers to apply 'for more details of attractions and forthcoming events', somewhat
curiously to inland Louth.

The Great Central is not a railway one normally associates with ships and the seaside,
but Immingham, Grimsby and Cleethorpes
are the great exceptions, although, curiously,
the Great Central also served New Brighton,
far away on the other side of England and exactly parallel with Grimsby. The Great Central's links with the east coast go back deep
into its Manchester, Sheffield & Lincolnshire
Railway days. Queen Victoria, no less, performed the Grimsby Dock Company's opening ceremony in 1852, docks which came into

existence directly as a result of the railway company's willingness to set up in joint competition with Hull docks, across the Humber, and the North Eastern Railway, which served them.

The Manchester, Sheffield & Lincolnshire Railway not only opened a fish dock at Grimsby, but also even became part owners of a fleet of fishing boats. Over the years many classes of locomotive were built especially for the fish traffic, types which had to be both powerful and fast in order to get the lengthy trains of fish vans to the inland markets as quickly as possible. When the MS&LR became the Great Central at the end of the nineteenth century, J.G. Robinson designed the Class '8' (later 'B5') 4-6-0s which were always known as the 'Fish Engines', whilst in LNER days there were the big boilered 'K3' 2-6-0s (originally a GNR design) and eventually the 'V2' 2-6-2s which were equally at home on express goods and express passenger trains.

In the late 1920s the LNER handled be-

tween 3,500 and 4,000 wagon loads of fish each week, two-thirds originating at Hull and Grimsby. The latter regularly supplied the extraordinary total of over 3,000 stations in England and Wales. Busiest day of all was the Wednesday before Good Friday in 1928 when 1,348 tons of fish was loaded into 272 wagons. There were five regular express fish trains, the rest being conveyed by ordinary passenger or goods train. In the late 1950s the Chairman of the Eastern Area Board announced that 'Grimsby docks, especially the fish docks, were a grave financial liability to the (British Transport) Commission'. The time was approaching when fish traffic conveyed by rail would be the exception rather than the rule.

Cleethorpes, which the coming of the railway had turned from a fishing village into a resort, has proved better equipped to cope with the changing decades of the latter part of the present century than Grimsby, not least perhaps because its station is set beside the beach in as convenient a position as any railway company could possibly desire. Cleethorpes is directly linked to a considerable number of destinations: Doncaster, Sheffield,

Cleethorpes on a May evening in 1982.

Manchester, Liverpool, Nottingham, Derby, Birmingham and London, the latter by an HST named train, the 'Humber-Lincs'. This leaves Cleethorpes at 6.20 am, calls at Grimsby Town eight minutes later, leaves Lincoln Central at 7.24, and reaches King's Cross at 9.20, the 183½ miles taking exactly 180 minutes. But the days of regular summer seaside specials are a thing of the past, the frequent ordinary services considered sufficient for the needs of day-trippers and holidaymakers.

Humberside and the Wolds

Hull is a good bit further up the Humber than Grimsby; the most direct link between the two used to be by train from Grimsby to New Holland Pier and then by ferry to Hull, a service which saw the last active Sealink paddle-steamers. The building of the great Humber road bridge sounded the death knell of this service and one of the paddlers is now

moored beneath the bridge. Hull was certainly never seaside but it was, of course, and even now still is, a major port, and as such was served by an extensive network of railways. Much of this was owned by the mighty North Eastern Railway but a significant proportion belonged to the Hull & Barnsley, a concern which possessed but one main line linking the centres from which it took its name.

When I visited Kingston upon Hull, to give it its proper name, in 1983, I found it a sad city, stricken by unemployment and much of the old docks derelict, although the most historic parts were being restored. Little of the Hull & Barnsley system remains.

Humbersiders' nearest seaside resorts proper are at Withernsea and Hornsea and the NER owned both the branches which connected them with Hull. The former opened as an independent line in 1856, despite the ceremonial marquee collapsing on invited guests, and was taken over by the NER four years later, whilst the Hull & Hornsea Railway began operations in March 1864. Misfortune also accompanied this event, the inspecting officer, a Colonel Rich, falling off a bridge into the water at one point. Perhaps a jinx was at work, or suspected to be, for neither Withernsea nor Hornsea ever really developed. Poor receipts forced the Directors of the Hornsea railway to sell out to the NER in 1866. Today, neither resort gets a mention in the current Michelin guide, and Beeching did away with both branches, all traffic coming to an end on 19 October 1964.

Hull, being, like so many East Coast towns and cities, very flat, once abounded in level crossings. Philip Larkin, who was the university librarian at Hull, wrote 'Whitsun Weddings', which describes a journey from Hull to King's Cross in steam days, and is perhaps the best known of all his works. It begins thus:

'That Whitsun, I was late getting away:
Not till about
One-twenty on the sunlit Saturday
Did my three-quarters empty train pull out,

All windows down, all cushions hot, all sense
Of being in a hurry gone. We ran
Behind the backs of houses, crossed a street
Of blinding windscreens, smelt the fishdock; thence
The river's level drifting breadth began
Where sky and Lincolnshire and water meet.'

The one other line linking Hull with the coast was the oldest. This was the one from Bridlington, a George Hudson line, which opened in November 1846 and encompassed in its 31 miles the astonishing total of 37 level crossings. Bridlington has a long history and featured prominently in the Civil War when the Parliamentary fleet bombarded it. It acquired a reputation as a rather select watering place in the early part of the nineteenth century, but once the railway arrived in 1842 the workers from the industrial West Riding discovered and popularized it. To the north it was linked to Scarborough but most of its traffic approached from the south, either from Humberside or from Doncaster, Sheffield, Leeds, Bradford, Halifax *et al*, by way of Market Weighton and Driffield. The sands, the harbour, where many fishermen found

there were greater profits to be made giving joy rides around the bay, and all the traditional delights of a large English seaside resort brought the visitors pouring in. Today the population of Bridlington is close on 30,000.

Bridlington had its own loco shed and although it was a small, three-road affair there was accommodation for the many locomotives which brought in seaside extras to rest over, and these might range, even in the late 1950s, from former NER 4–6–0s, through 'D49s', 'K3s' and 'B1s' to Stanier '5MTs'. The 9.5 am Hull to Bridlington and Scarborough was so popular that it would sometimes run in five portions, each of ten carriages. The LNER was hard put to find sufficient carriages, and corridor stock was something of a luxury. When one considers how many cars one would need to accommodate the 4–5,000 passengers those five trains carried, it is little wonder that our roads are so congested.

Today Bridlington station is still quite extensive and Quay Crossing signal box continues to function, controlling LNER-type semaphores, but the dock lines are gone, a coach park occupies much of the yard, and summer extras have all but disappeared. The direct line from Selby and the west through

Left Bridlington shed in about 1960 with 'K3s', 'B1s', a 'B16' and a Stanier '5MT' waiting to take charge of return excursion trains. (*Author's collection*)

Right No 4468 *Mallard* beneath the famous gantry at Scarborough in July 1988.

Market Weighton to Driffield closed in the mid-1950s, so through trains have now to take the less direct route by way of the Hull suburbs.

The final 22 miles of the Hull to Scarborough line is much the most picturesque. The scenery changes dramatically as the Wolds reach out to the sea to form Flamborough Head, celebrated for its variety of sea birds. The railway north of Bridlington, now single track, is less used than the southern section, and climbs steeply with views across the neat red brick houses of north Bridlington to the sea some half-mile away. It then curves through the disused Flamborough station, closed in 1970, and swings first one way then another through rolling countryside all the way past Filey to Scarborough. The section from Hunmanby is double track so both platforms at Filey station are in use.

Filey has fine sands, spectacular cliffs and an equable climate, and from the early 1800s began to attract visitors — the holiday camp came later. It's a quite small, elegant, scenic resort, popular with those who like golf, gardens, sailing and peace and quiet. The dozen or so trains in each direction are handy for those wanting to avoid the razzmatazz which is to be had at Scarborough, a quarter of an hour's ride away. Seamer, where the branch joins the main line from York, is now the only station open between Filey and Scarborough, which means that caravans and donkeys graze undisturbed at Gristhorpe and Cayton, the former closing in 1959, the latter seven years earlier.

Scarborough fliers

Scarborough station looks rather grander from the outside than it does from within, although its recent refurbishment means that all of it is in good order. It has an ornate, Italianate, domed tower and three stone pediments beneath, which echo the big, black, Doric, Westborough Methodist church up the road; the architect of this must surely have been an admirer of the Euston arch. The station's roof is supported by a plethora of brightly painted iron beams and spans, although much of the platform area is uncovered. The very long platform 1, extended by the LNER in 1934, has an awning for part of its length. It is here that steam excursions pull in from York and Hull. The station is also well endowed with a

fine selection of semaphore signals, including a gantry spanning the approach to the station. This gantry has been used of late as a symbol of Scarborough's railways in various pieces of promotional literature; I wonder if it would be possible when it is eventually replaced by colour lights to leave it in place without causing confusion to drivers? Falsgrave signal box, which now controls all Scarborough's movements, the station one having been demolished, stands on the end of the platform, and behind it buffer stops block the entrance to Falsgrave tunnel through which trains on the coast line to Whitby used to pass.

Scarborough claims to be the oldest seaside resort in the country, something Brighton disputes, but certainly visitors did come to sample the sea breezes and walk on the magnificent sands some time before the railway arrived from York. The bathing machine first made its appearance at Scarborough, Charlotte Brontë died here, and the castle dates back to Roman times. There is some magnificent Victorian architecture of various shapes and sizes, the fishing fleet still sails from the harbour, donkeys plod up and down the sands past astonishingly ingenious and spectacular seafood displays, two-horse carriages and vintage open-top buses ply the promenade and a cliff tramway operates behind a vast Victorian hotel owned by Butlins. In short, Scarborough is the biggest and possibly the finest resort on the East Coast of England.

Steam enthusiasts owe a particular debt to Scarborough, for the town council has provided funds, notably for a turntable, to enable the likes of *Mallard, City of Truro, Duchess of Hamilton, Sir Lamiel* and many other famous locomotives to work excursions into the town. These run, not just for enthusiasts, but also as much, if not more, for families, and make it possible to re-create the excitement which earlier generations knew of travelling at reasonable cost by steam train for a day out by the sea.

Goods traffic has vanished from Scarborough, the depot and sidings having become a bus and car park, and the line which used to run along the coast through Robin Hood's Bay to Whitby closed in 1965. Trains taking this route had to reverse out of Scarborough station and then head back under the town and away to the north. This line, opened in 1885, was made up almost entirely of fearsome gradients, which was tough on those who had to operate it but grand for the passenger who was afforded magnificent views both out across the North Sea and in-

land over the moors. There was much regret when the line closed. It was for long associated with Wilson Worsdell's 'W' Class 4–6–0 tanks, rebuilt by Raven as 4–6–2Ts and classified 'A6' by the LNER. They were known locally as 'Willies', not surprisingly with all those 'W' associations, and were largely replaced in the 1930s by 'A8' Class 4–6–2Ts. These were also of NER origin, having been built with the rare 4–4–4T wheel arrangement.

The year 1965 was pretty miserable for railway buffs in Whitby. Not only did they lose their link with Scarborough but the line to York, which joined the York to Scarborough route just beyond Malton at Rillington, also saw its last train. Well, not entirely. In 1967 the North Yorkshire Moors Railway Company was set up with the intention of reopening the section from Pickering to Grosmont. This was a highly picturesque piece of railway, running through a national

Above Stanier 'Pacific' No 46229 *Duchess of Hamilton* makes a spectacular exit from Scarborough with the 'Yorkshire Coast Express' in April 1985.

Left NER-built 'Atlantic' No 706 and 'D49' 4–4–0 No 258 *The Cattistock* wait outside Scarborough with returning excursion trains, August 1938. (*Colour-Rail*)

Right Former NER 'A8' 4–6–2T No 69861 at Beckhole with a train from Whitby in 1956. The leading carriage is also NER built. (*Colour-Rail*)

An express from Whitby and Scarborough arriving at King's Cross behind 4–4–0 No 4343 and 'Atlantic' No 4418, 13 August 1937. (*Author's collection*)

park, and at Grosmont it connected with the Whitby to Middlesbrough line, Whitby's last remaining rail link. Subsequently, the 18 miles between Grosmont and Pickering re-entered the land of the living in 1973.

Occasionally an NYMR locomotive is permitted to work over BR metals to Whitby, but the recent singling of the line and the removal of all signals between Grosmont and Whitby has not helped and BR does not seem to be able to make up its mind whether it really wants to encourage what would surely be a lucrative venture for both parties if regular steam working could return to Whitby.

Whitby station is superbly situated in the centre of the town beside the harbour and within sight of the sea. Its most attractive feature is a handsome tiled map of the NER system, one of a number still to be found in former NER territory — Scarborough and

York, for example, each have one. Otherwise it is pretty run down, and although BR and the council have plans to improve it and its surroundings they seem in no hurry to do so.

At one time the LNER carried 70 per cent of all the fish landed in mainland Britain and Whitby played its part in this trade. However, as long ago as 1900 there were complaints that despite 'its railway facilities with lines in four directions ... the industry has fallen away sadly, and the Harbour Board seem greatly to blame'. Visitors were said to be the town's principal source of income although the season was very short 'from mid-July to the middle of September' which was much regretted as in June 'everything is at its best, and the hedges are covered with wild roses and woodbine'. Today, although few visitors use the train, they certainly come almost all the year round and I have seen the town packed out on a wet Easter Bank Holiday Sunday.

Whitby's one surviving line, to Middlesbrough, has been marketed of late as the Esk Valley line. Passenger figures have gone

up markedly, as well they might, for the 30 odd miles are pure delight through quite magnificent scenery. The stations, mostly unstaffed, are quaint, although none can compare with Battersby Junction. Here the

Above The 14.20 to Darlington leaving Whitby on 8 April 1985.

Below Former GWR 0–6–2T No 6619 south of Goathland on the North Yorks Moors Railway in March 1986.

Left The North Eastern coastline, Whitby station, March 1985.

Below right East Coast express — Deltic No 55022 *Royal Scots Grey* accelerates through Wood Green with the inaugural down 'Silver Jubilee', 8 June 1977.

DMUs reverse, although once there was a through route to the now freight-only North-allerton to Stockton line. When I was last there in 1986, Battersby sported an attractive NER signal box, a fine array of semaphore signals, including a North Eastern Railway fixed distant, and even possessed a water tower complete with flexible pipe.

A spectacular piece of railway architecture is the 915-foot Larpool viaduct which used to carry the Scarborough to Whitby, Saltburn, Redcar and Middlesbrough line over the Grosmont to Whitby line on the outskirts of the town. It is said to contain 5 million bricks, although I've never met anyone who counted them.

Teesside

The closure of the line from Scarborough to Whitby and Middlesbrough deprived our rail network of one of its most scenic routes. To quote P.W.B. Semmens writing in *Trains Illustrated* in April 1951, 'In places, a stone thrown from the carriage would land in the sea several hundred feet below the train'. There were tunnels and viaducts in profusion and fierce gradients all the way; Semmens remarks, 'indeed for the whole way to Stainton Dale (penultimate station before Scarborough) the speed only twice reached 40 mph'. The section from Saltburn to Whitby closed in 1958, although freight continues to run beyond Saltburn as far as the Cleveland Potash works at Boulby atop the highest cliffs in England. The Whitby to Scarborough section closed in 1965.

Saltburn was developed by industrialist Henry Pease some hundred years ago. His Saltburn Improvement Company turned the fishing village into a resort, helped by the NER which arrived in 1861. Always a terminus — trains continuing south-east along the coast had to reverse out — Saltburn station has lost the roof over its two platforms but retains its frontage. The Zetland Hotel used to be owned by the NER. As at Scarborough there is a cliff railway which links the station with the sands below. An excellent half-hourly DMU service runs between Saltburn, Redcar, Middlesbrough (just over 30 minutes away), Darlington and Bishop Auckland.

From here until we are clear of Tyneside, the coast is deeply industrial, although there are beaches and various pleasure facilities fighting for survival amongst the commercial harbours, the coal staithes, the steel works, nuclear power stations, scrapyards, chemical works etc, and indeed winning the struggle now that industry is receding.

Many people expect to find their seaside at the end of a journey through rolling green and yellow fields and today they are prepared to go a long way to find it. But in the nineteenth and early twentieth centuries it was the resorts close to the great industrial and mercantile centres, that could be reached with the

minimum of time and expenditure, which flourished, where every minute of the few precious days away from the mill, the works, or the mine counted. Time and money spent travelling was begrudged and thus Southend, New Brighton, Hartlepool, Whitley Bay, Bray, Bangor and the Clyde resorts reached the heights of their popularity.

Redcar is one such. Lying close to the mouth of the Tees, its latest steel works dates back only as far as the mid-1970s. Yet Redcar is a true resort, and still a popular one, with natural breakwaters which ensure a fine bathing beach, gardens, terraces, a racecourse and all manner of entertainment. The half-hourly DMUs to Middlesbrough, 18 minutes away, and Saltburn, 15 minutes distant, call at the two-platform, somewhat unkempt Central station with its overall roof. Redcar possesses two other stations, Redcar East and British Steel Redcar.

West of Redcar the line plunges deep into industrial Teesside, running close to the river to Middlesbrough, a busy, though only two-platform, station, largely rebuilt after suffering bomb damage during the Second World War. Apart from the many DMUs which frequent it there is a daily HST working to and

from King's Cross. Named the 'Cleveland Executive', it takes 3 hours 9 minutes to cover the 240 miles. At Eaglescliffe, the next station to Thornaby, the 'Cleveland Executive' reverses and heads through Stockton, birthplace, along with Darlington, of the world's public railway systems. It continues along the north bank of the Tees to Seaton Carew and Hartlepool.

West Hartlepool, a town of almost 100,000 inhabitants, and which of late has dropped its prefix, existed long before the Industrial Revolution, as an Anglo-Saxon settlement and a port, although it was the coal trade which brought about its prosperity. Seaton Carew developed as the select end of Hartlepool with high-class hotels, a promenade and seafront.

North of Hartlepool the scenery grows considerably more rural. Evidence of coal mining, past and present, alternates with views of fields and beaches through Seaham and on to Sunderland. Despite the predominance of the shipbuilding and coal industries, Sunderland, a town of almost a quarter of a million inhabitants, possesses beaches, promenades and all manner of entertainments, though to class it as a resort is, I agree, pushing it a bit.

The present line along the coast from Stockton to Sunderland originated as a whole collection of independent lines, some of them colliery ones, and although the oldest section dates from 1830, it was not completed until 1905 when the final section, from Horden to Seaham, was built by the NER. This section cost some £250,000 to build, which was considered a great deal of money at the time. It was largely accounted for by the many viaducts and embankments necessary to carry the line over the ravines, or denes, which *The Railway Magazine* of April 1903 described as 'nearly all well wooded and forming a delightful contrast to the surrounding country, which, swept by constant gales from the sea, is generally bleak and desolate'. The expense of such a line was justified, firstly by 'certain coal owners . . . desirous of sinking pits under the sea' and the North Eastern Railway being 'ready to convey the coal as soon as the mines are developed', and also to give 'an alternative route from Newcastle and Sunderland to Hartlepool, Stockton, and thence to Manchester and Liverpool, with better gradients and curves than their present route'. Of the eight stations once in use be-

Above A Sunderland to Middlesbrough train at Hartlepool on 22 January 1987. (*Dr M. Rhodes*)

Below DMUs heading to and from Sunderland crossing the High Level Bridge at Newcastle, August 1979.

tween Hartlepool and Sunderland, only Seaham remains open. The line was one of the first to be dieselized, DMUs replacing 'V1' and 'V3' 2-6-2Ts and the odd remaining NER-built 'G5' 0-4-4T in November 1955.

Colliery lines usually operated passenger services for their workers, and typical of these was the South Shields, Marsden & Whitburn Colliery Railway. It almost, but not quite, connected with the Newcastle to South Shields BR line. Whilst this had been electrified by the LNER in 1938, the colliery passengers were still being trundled along the shores of Marsden Bay as late as 1953 in ex-Great Eastern and Great North of Scotland Railway six-wheel carriages dating from the previous century 'stripped of all interior partitions and fittings, wooden seats substituted, and as all the platforms are on the seaward side the door handles of the older coaches are removed from the other side and the drop-windows boarded up'. This picture of archaic ob-

Former North Eastern Railway 'H1' Class 4-4-4T, LNER No 2144, at Newcastle Central, 13 June 1933. (*Madgwick*)

solescence was completed by the motive power, a Robert Stephenson-built 0-6-0 purchased from the North Eastern Railway who had themselves acquired it in 1856! Ancient as its rolling-stock was, this particular colliery line was hardly unique, and many veteran former main line locomotives and carriages found similar employment.

Tyne to the Border

At the turn of the century the vastly busy North Tyneside lines of the North Eastern Railway from Newcastle out to the coast carried close on 10 million passengers each year. Then in 1902 the rival tramways were electrified and in a little over two years the number of passengers travelling by train was almost halved. Disastrous as this was for the NER, it was not unexpected and plans for a comeback were already being prepared. Electrification for both street and suburban railway travel was all the rage in the first decade of this century and contributed much towards the improvement of conditions in town and city centres and the blossoming of

suburbs throughout the land. The North Eastern, a most progressive railway, became the first main-line company in Britain — just — to adopt electric traction when multiple units began to carry passengers on 29 March 1904, the complete service between Newcastle Central and the coast beginning in July that year.

The third rail system was used, 74 vehicles were built at the company's York workshops — 39 motor-coaches, 33 trailers and two motor luggage vans — and in all 80.4 track miles and 37 route miles were electrified. Of open layout with clerestory roofs, the trains

were painted in a striking livery of red and cream. Tynesiders loved them. By 1913 the number of passengers carried had climbed above the record 1901 figure. Expresses ran between the coast and the city centre not only in the mornings and back again in the evenings — except on Saturdays when they came back at midday — but also at lunchtimes on Mondays to Fridays so that businessmen could come home for a meal; others operated for the convenience of theatre-goers in the evenings. The ordinary stopping trains ran every half-hour and on Saturday afternoons and Sundays trippers took the place of

NER Tyneside electric.

businessmen and flocked to the sands of Tynemouth and Whitley Bay in their thousands.

Tynemouth and Whitley Bay are splendid resorts with magnificent sands and the arrival of the railway brought trippers flocking to them from the crowded terraces of Newcastle and Gateshead. Tynemouth is a grand place, with tall, handsome Victorian buildings set up on the cliffs looking out over the North Sea past the ruins of the ancient Priory and Castle. The station began as a terminus, the line being extended from Shields — as North Shields was then known — in 1847. There were two railways serving the coast at this time, the Blyth & Tyne and the North Eastern. Eventually the latter took over the former and rebuilt and improved the complicated series of lines linking Newcastle city centre and the coast to form the familiar present-day circular route. The company architect, William Bell, designed a magnificent station of 25 bays of ridge and furrow glazed roofs, supported by splendid Gothic ironwork, covering two through and six excursion bay platforms.

I had no expectation of finding anything much out of the ordinary when I first visited Whitley Bay station and therefore the glories of its extensive iron and glasswork, similar though far from identical to Tynemouth, were all the more delightful. The same cannot be said of its train service at that time. The electric services inaugurated by the North Eastern Railway had prospered and in the mid 1930s

the LNER decided to electrify the service along the south bank of the Tyne from Newcastle Central to South Shields. Thirty-six of the NER-built vehicles were refurbished for the South Tyneside line whilst for the North Tyneside services Metro-Cammell was given a contract to build 64 twin-car articulated units plus two parcels vans. These latter bore a distinct resemblance to the Liverpool Street-Shenfield and the Manchester area EMUs designed by the LNER, but were delayed by the war and were not put into service until early BR days.

The detailed history of the Tyneside electric stock is complicated, not least because of a disastrous fire at the Walker Gate depot in 1918 in which 34 cars were destroyed, necessitating replacements. Newest of all, although hardly the most advanced in design, were 15 two-car units and a parcels van, built at Eastleigh in 1955 and of typically Southern appearance with slam doors and no communication between carriages. There were also rakes of former steam stock, and a perhaps unique facility, Perambulator Vans. These were converted vehicles, especially adapted to carry mums and dads and their small offspring in their prams and pushchairs on their way to the seaside, and ran on summer Saturdays and Sundays attached to ordinary trains.

The South Tyneside passenger electrics were retired in 1963, being replaced by slower diesel multiple units and the final blow, or so it seemed at the time, fell in 1967. British

Railways announced, referring to 'recent criticism concerning the proposed change to diesel traction on North Tyneside . . . The North Tyneside electric services have lost money heavily for some time and diesels enable us to reduce running costs. New stock suitable for the existing third rail system would be expensive and we have available diesel cars eminently suitable to operate over these lines.'

And so the Tyneside electrics, which had carried generations between the seaside, the docks, the shipyards, the suburbs and the city centre for over 60 years disappeared, giving way to a motley collection of slower, far less 'eminently suitable' diesels. Such a retrograde move at a time when the ever-increasing congestion and pollution of cities throughout the world was causing acute heart-searchings and was prompting many gradiose relief schemes, all of them centred around swift, clean and efficient electric rail travel, seemed extraordinarily short-sighted. Yet, within 15 years Tyneside would be able to boast just such a system, the most up to date in the British Isles.

Newcastle is further from London than any other city in England, even if HSTs cover the 268 miles in a fraction over three hours, and it has a highly developed sense of indepen-

On the Newcastle Metro, July 1983.

dence. At around the time BR ended electrification on North Tyneside a newly created body, the Tyneside Passenger Transport Executive, set up a study into local transport and came up with the solution of the Metro, an electric railway system, using much of the former electrified system but tunnelling under the city to provide a number of stations in the heart of the shopping and business quarters, including, of course, one at Newcastle Central. Work began in the autumn of 1974, the first section, from Haymarket to Tynemouth, began operation in 1980, and it was completed, out to South Shields, in March 1984.

The little yellow and white four-car trains must surely be the precursors of many throughout the land if our cities are not to grind to a halt.

Beyond the great resorts of Tynemouth and Whitley Bay the NER had branches extending up the coast to Blyth, North Blyth, Newbiggin-by-the-Sea and Amble. The first three are still open to freight but closed to passenger traffic in 1964. The Amble branch closed as long ago as 1930. Although they are industrial towns associated with the coal trade and shipping, they also have fine sandy beaches, so typical of the East Coast, and Amble has developed into something of a yachting centre.

Approaching the Scots border, the East Coast Main Line really does live up to its name as it comes within sight of the North Sea. The last branch before the border, to the picturesque fishing port of Seahouses, closed in 1951, and so, past Tweedmouth and over the celebrated Royal Border Bridge, which the *Wonder Book of Railways* used to love featuring in the 1930s with a Gresley 'Pacific' steaming across it, to Berwick-on-Tweed.

The section from Newcastle to Berwick was opened in 1847 by the North Eastern Railway who found that the North British had arrived the year before from Edinburgh. The NER, discovering Berwick's ancient castle to be in its way had, naturally enough, demolished it but had very decently incorporated some of the stones in its station, so not all was lost.

EASTERN SCOTLAND

Across the Border

Because the Border between England and Scotland is set at so steep an angle, Berwick is surprisingly far north, way up beyond Carlisle which is parallel with Newcastle, 68 miles south of Berwick on the East Coast main line, and is beyond Ayr and level with the Clyde coast resorts. When West Coast expresses changed their LNWR engines at Carlisle the Caledonian would have charge for over 100 miles, but from Berwick to Edinburgh it is little more than 50 miles. When the East Coast route was established, the partners agreed that North Eastern Railway locomotives would continue right through to Edinburgh and thus the traveller at Waverley station would normally find one of Raven's impressive 'Atlantics', rather than an equally imposing Reid 4–4–2 of the North British, at the head of his Anglo-Scottish express.

The Edinburgh to Berwick line had opened on a hot, sunny midsummer day in 1846, celebrated, naturally enough, by a beanfeast in a marquee at Dunbar, a seaside town once the scene of a number of battles, later a fishing port, and now a holiday and golfing resort.

So closely does the Berwick to Edinburgh line hug the coast that there was only ever

'D49' 4–4–0 No 62729 *Rutlandshire* leaving Edinburgh with a stopping train to North Berwick. 'A3' 'Pacific' No 60068 *Sir Visto* is alongside with a Newcastle express. 8 June 1960.

"THE CORONATION"
ON THE EAST COAST ENTERING SCOTLAND
IT'S QUICKER BY RAIL
FULL INFORMATION FROM ANY L·N·E·R OFFICE OR AGENCY

Left A Frank H. Mason poster for the LNER.

Right Preserved NBR 0-6-0 *Maude* at Rainhill, 1980.

Below right Scottish preservation. An industrial 0-4-0T bustles into Bo'ness station with a former LNER non-corridor brake composite. In the other platform is NER saloon No 461. September 1982.

room for three branch lines off it in the seaward direction, all very short. That from Burnmouth to Eyemouth, an ancient port which still has a fishing fleet, closed in 1962, the Drem to North Berwick line remains open, whilst the nearby branch to Gullane closed back in 1932.

Today Dunbar is the only station open between Drem, 18 miles out of Edinburgh and the junction for the North Berwick line, and the Border, the other eight having been closed over the years. North Berwick is served by around a dozen trains in each direction daily, DMUs to and from Haymarket, a few continuing over the Forth Bridge to Cowdenbeath or Cardenden. The journey between Edinburgh Waverley and North Berwick, stopping at Prestonpans, Longniddry and Drem, takes 33 minutes. North Berwick, like so many seaside places on Scotland's east coast, is a mecca for the golfer, the most famous of the courses in the vicinity being the world's oldest at Muirfield.

Edinburgh, like Glasgow, is not quite seaside itself, although it is close enough for the Forth Bridge and the whole of the Forth estuary to be visible from Arthur's Seat, the extinct volcano overlooking Waverley station.

Being a smaller and far less industrial city than Glasgow, it never developed comparably extensive suburban or seaside services. Many of the suburban lines there have largely disappeared and the complex railway networks the North British and the Caledonian Railways built, often in a spirit of rivalry rather than out of commercial necessity, around the docks at Leith have been greatly simplified.

Leith as a port was at one time second only to Glasgow in Scotland and still handles a variety of cargoes and ships including some very large ones. So important were Leith docks that the first line to serve them was opened to Edinburgh in 1838, before the Scottish capital was linked to Glasgow. It was built to the curious gauge of 4 ft 6 ins, but was soon converted to the standard 4 ft 8½ ins when the NBR took it over in 1844. Our chief interest in the lines around Leith is that they formed part of the East Coast route to Dundee and Aberdeen, connecting with ferries across the Forth and the Tay estuaries.

The Edinburgh & Northern Railway opened in May 1848 and by using a ferry from Granton, adjoining Leith, to Burntisland and another from Tayport and Broughty Ferry, the through route from London by way of

Edinburgh to Dundee was established. The first public train ferry in the world was designed by Thomas Bouch and inaugurated on the Firth of Forth in 1850. Fish was a most important traffic from the earliest days; indeed, the presence of a thriving fish port often prompted the building of a railway to it, and Bouch's ferry regularly shipped fish wagons. A similar ferry was put into service on the Tay, and both ran until they were replaced by bridges.

The Tay and Forth bridges are amongst the most famous in the world, the former because of the disaster which befell it, the latter because of its overpowering grandeur. One of the most photographed structures in the world, I've not yet seen a picture of the Forth Bridge which has done it justice. The best concentrate on detail and thus give some idea of its enormous size. However familiar its image, nothing quite prepares one for the truly astonishing manner in which it dominates the land and seascape in which it stands. It is not merely beautiful or elegant,

though it possesses both these qualities. The Forth Bridge is simply tremendous, and after 100 years still inspires awe that mere mortals could have conceived and executed such a vast undertaking.

It was Bouch, the designer of the first successful train ferries, who designed the first, ill-fated Tay bridge. When it collapsed in December 1879 not only did it take to their immediate deaths the unfortunate passengers and crew of the train passing over it, but it just as surely killed Bouch, the shock of the accident and the blame heaped upon him for faulty design and poor supervision of the construction work bringing about his death. The stumps of his bridge can still be seen sticking up alongside the second bridge, erected in 1887.

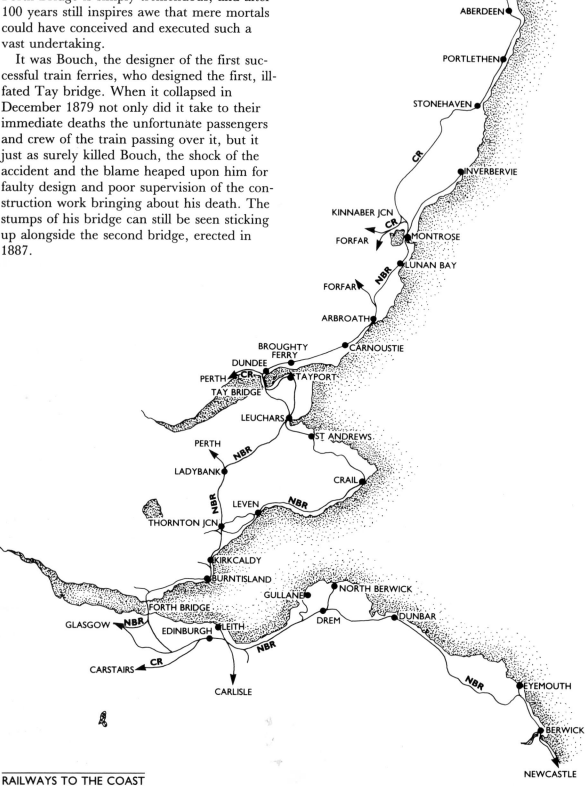

The completion of the Forth Bridge in 1890, a joint work funded by the Great Northern, North Eastern, Midland and North British railway companies, consolidated the East Coast route and brought it down to 524 miles from King's Cross to Aberdeen, or 538 from St Pancras to Aberdeen, for the Midland with its Settle and Carlisle route was a serious rival for Anglo-Scottish traffic.

The Forth Bridge carries the main line across to the Fife shore, between Rosyth and Inverkeithing, whence it continues along the

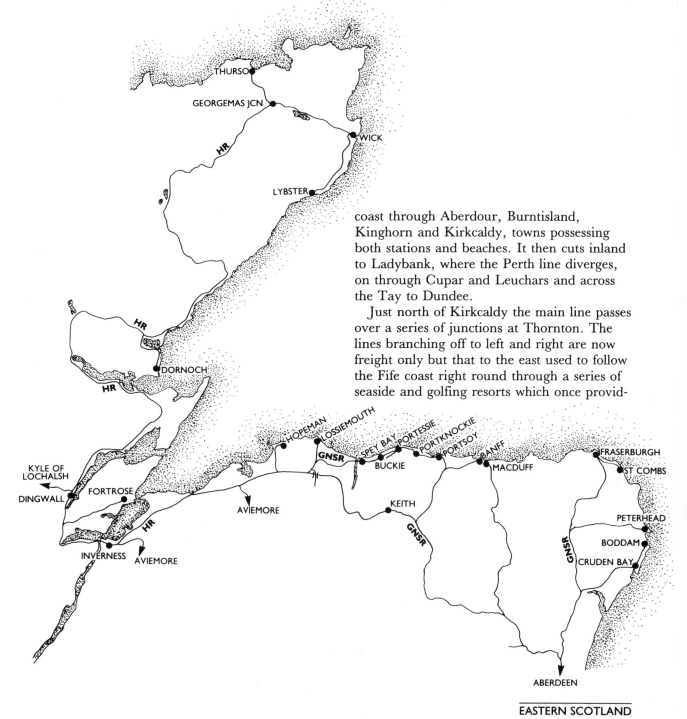

coast through Aberdour, Burntisland, Kinghorn and Kirkcaldy, towns possessing both stations and beaches. It then cuts inland to Ladybank, where the Perth line diverges, on through Cupar and Leuchars and across the Tay to Dundee.

Just north of Kirkcaldy the main line passes over a series of junctions at Thornton. The lines branching off to left and right are now freight only but that to the east used to follow the Fife coast right round through a series of seaside and golfing resorts which once provid-

EASTERN SCOTLAND

ed the North British and the London & North Eastern Railway companies with much business. Leven, Lundin Links, St Monans, Anstruther, Crail and St Andrews are all either small resorts, fishing villages or golfing centres which were served by the railway; much the most famous was St Andrews, but for all its fame and distinction, British Rail closed both the station and the line passing through it in 1969.

The St Andrews branch rejoined the main line at Leuchars Junction, whence a further

Above A Class '27' on a Dundee to Edinburgh train meets a Class '37' and a Class '20' on a coal train on the Forth Bridge in September 1982.

N.B. Railway.—Express leaving Edinburgh.

Left A NBR 'Atlantic' leaving Edinburgh Waverley with an Aberdeen express, *circa* 1922. (*Author's collection*)

Preserved 'A4' 'Pacific' No 60009 *Union of South Africa* about to set off from Perth for Edinburgh in May 1982.

branch, which closed in 1966 after the opening of the Tay road bridge, headed off to Tayport and then curved along the south bank of the Tay to rejoin the main line at Wormit, immediately south of the Tay Bridge.

Just before the junction with the main line, the Tayport branch passed through Wormit station. This closed in 1969, but the history of this until then rather obscure little seaside station was far from over. At the end of 1980 the Scottish Railway Preservation Society decided that it was just what it needed for its terminus at Bo'ness. It handed over a cheque for £300 to British Rail, got to work with cranes, saws, jacks, etc and, carefully dismantling the buildings, transported them south. Thus a North British wayside station, which had expected to end its days as it had begun them beside the Tay estuary, found itself transformed into the terminus of a preserved railway beside the Forth. Since their re-erection, the Wormit buildings have been married to an all-over roof which once stood at Waverley station, Edinburgh, and today the station plays host to a variety of unique locomotives and carriages, a living museum of Scottish railway history.

A Class '40' crossing the Tay Bridge. (*British Railways*)

Dundee and Aberdeen

At Dundee the old rivals, the North British and the Caledonian, renewed hostilities, and, to be fair, acquaintanceship too. The NBR came in over the Tay by means of the longest bridge in Britain, the CR along the north bank of the river from Perth. Dundee's first railway, from the inland town of Newtyle, was completed in 1831; this would become part of the Caledonian.

Dundee used to boast three principal passenger stations, West, East and Tay Bridge. West was a terminus belonging to the Caledonian Railway which served Perth and Glasgow Buchanan Street, whilst East, likewise a terminus, belonged to the joint company and was used by Arbroath trains. Neither ever did a vast amount of business and with the closure of stations and branch lines in the 1950s and '60s both became redundant and all trains now call at the always much busier Tay Bridge through station. Although not particularly well laid out in a cramped cutting which is actually below high-tide level, it is conveniently placed both for the waterfront and the city centre.

The first seaside line, out to Arbroath, was opened in 1838. Like the earliest Edinburgh line this was built to a non-standard gauge, 5 ft 6 ins, but the Dundee Harbour Trust, who owned it, soon converted it to 4 ft 8½ ins, and as such it became the joint property of the North British and the Caledonian companies. The fishing port of Arbroath specialized in the famous Arbroath 'smokie', and the holidaymakers flocked here so that a town of considerable substance grew up during the nineteenth century. It now has a population of around 24,000 and is the terminus of a commuter service from Dundee. The 16-mile journey, much of it within sight of the sea, takes 33 minutes stopping at six intermediate stations; fast trains from Aberdeen do the journey non-stop in 20 minutes. All the stations serve the seaside, the most popular being Carnoustie with its celebrated golf course — next to it are Golf Street and Barry Links stations — and Broughty Ferry, a one-time

fishing village developed into a resort at the mouth of the Tay opposite Tayport.

The lightly graded Arbroath line kept its North British 'C16' 4–4–2s for several decades, and ex-Caledonian 0–4–4Ts shared duties with them until the early days of nationalisation. The service has been operated by DMUs for many years now, but in addition the discerning commuter can travel on an East Coast Aberdeen to Edinburgh and King's Cross HST if he consults the timetable carefully; up on the 08.54 from Arbroath, for example, returning home perhaps after a bit of overtime on the 19.13 out of Dundee.

Beyond Arbroath the coast line turns away from the sea; a Caledonian branch used to diverge inland to Forfar, whilst the main line, now exclusively former North British property, cuts behind the headland and comes back to the sea at Lunan Bay; the station here was closed long ago by the LNER in 1930. Beyond is Montrose, one of only three stations still surviving between Arbroath and Aberdeen.

Montrose is almost surrounded by water, set between the North Sea and the two-mile-square Montrose Basin, over which the station looks. Long a port, it became a spa in the early 1800s and developed into a full-fledged resort with the help of the NBR. A branch used to carry on up the coast to the small manufacturing town of Inverbervie; it closed in 1951.

North of Montrose there used to be one of the most famous junctions on the British railway network. This was Kinnaber. Here the Caledonian main line from the south by way of Perth and Forfar met the North British route. During the London to Aberdeen races between the East and West Coast rivals in the summer of 1895, whichever train reached Kinnaber Junction first had won, for the final 36 miles into Aberdeen were shared. The signalman at Kinnaber would wait eagerly for the bell to ring from either the next Caledonian or North British box down the line; as he was a Caledonian employee, we may have little doubt where his hopes lay. With the closure of the Forfar line by British

'Deltic' No 55014 *The Duke of Wellington's Regiment* at dusk north of Cove beside the North Sea on the last leg of its journey from King's Cross to Aberdeen, 4 November 1981. (*C.J.M. Lofthus*)

Rail, Kinnaber Junction became just a memory, and all trains from Glasgow and Perth now travel via Dundee.

Stonehaven, the last but one surviving station before Aberdeen, and 16 miles south of the Granite City, is situated on the edge of the town. The fishing fleet has gone, replaced by pleasure boats, but Stonehaven has a population of around 8,000, which increases considerably in the summer when the visitors arrive to sample the delights of the promenade, swim in the heated open-air pool, visit the Tolbooth Museum prison and take in a tour of a local distillery. Further north is Portlethen, much smaller than Stonehaven, but offering fishing and pleasure boating, a shingle beach and a railway station which is very well served by practically all Dundee-Aberdeen trains.

It is a curious thing that the final 36 miles of the East Coast route from King's Cross to Aberdeen should be over former Caledonian/LMS metals. True, the station was jointly owned by the LMS and the LNER after the Grouping but this was because of the presence of the Great North of Scotland, not the North British. The GN&SR had its own goods station, Waterloo, down in the docks

and its headquarters offices were also in Aberdeen, in Guild Street beside the station where there was also a hotel.

In the early 1970s Aberdeen became the oil capital of the British Isles and, not surprisingly, very prosperous, but it had always been a progressive seaport. Looking north-eastwards towards Scandinavia it has something of the air of a Viking city. Its publicity department likes to call itself 'offshore capital of Europe, the northernmost great city of the European Community', and certainly it has never lacked self-confidence. Before the oil boom, much of Aberdeen's business revolved around the fishing industry, and it is still the third busiest fishing port in Great Britain, something it may be grateful for after the oil runs out.

Southerners possibly do not have an image of Aberdeen as a holiday resort but it most certainly is. Ian Jack, the journalist and author, born and brought up beside the Clyde to the 'soundtrack of distant goods trains' describes his family's first seaside holiday in

Above North British-built 'J37' 0–6–0 No 64608 pulls out of Inverbervie with the branch's daily pick-up goods, July 1964. (*Michael Mensing/Colour-Rail*)

Below Former North British 'C15' 4–4–2T, LNER No 9133, at Kittybrewster in September 1937. (*Colour-Rail*)

1956. 'We went by train (an express; high tea in the dining car) and then by bus to a grey suburb in the lee of a headland where the North Sea sucked and boiled.' Unfortunately his father when selecting the boarding house had ignored his mother's protestations that it 'did not carry the distinguishing asterisk which marked the approval of Aberdeen's Town Hall' and it turned out to be 'a change of buses away from the beach but very close to a fishmeal factory'. The family 'ate boiled and fried haddock for a week'. In between young Jack 'walked to the lighthouse and stared forlornly across the harbour mouth at the inaccessible beach'.

The dining car express in which Ian Jack travelled to Aberdeen would, being ex-LMS, as likely as not have been in the charge of a Stanier Class '5' 4–6–0, but East Coast expresses went in for rather grander motive

power, as did the Glasgow trains at the very end of the steam era. The Edinburgh–Aberdeen was not an easy line to work with some heavy gradients, many curves, fierce sea winds and, to quote the RCTS History of the Locomotives of the LNER, 'lubrication of the rails by drips from the preceding fish train!'; big, powerful locomotives were always the order of the day. The NBR Reid 'Atlantics', LNER Classes 'C10/11', had a virtual monopoly from their introduction in 1906 until their withdrawal in the 1930s, by which time Gresley 'Pacifics' were on the Aberdeen road in some numbers. Possibly the most glamorous of all was the only class of 2–8–2 ever to run in passenger service in these islands. Six 'P2' 2–8–2s were built by Gresley in the mid-1930s especially for the Edinburgh–Aberdeen expresses. They were impressive-looking, immensely powerful locomotives and could keep time with anything the operating department cared to put behind them. Later, Gresley 'A4s', and their Peppercorn successors, the 'A2s', outliving all British 'Pacifics' except for Bulleid's,

Two North British-built 4–4–0s at the head of the 'Northern Belle' land-cruise train *circa* 1938. (*Author's collection*)

A Class '37' arrives at Inverness with a train from Wick and Thurso, August 1984.

held out on the Aberdeen line against the all-conquering diesels until late 1966.

The Far North

Most of the coastal area of north-east Scotland between Aberdeen and Inverness was the preserve of the Great North of Scotland Railway. This was probably the least known of all British railway companies, both on account of its remoteness from London and its small size. Its main line from Aberdeen as far as Keith, whence it connected with the Highland Railway, still exists, as does a now freight-only section of the branch from there which used to run down the valley of the Spey to Boat of Garten, but everything else is gone. At Keith the GNSR handed over its trains to the HR which conducted them on to Inverness, and today eight through trains run in each direction over the 108¼ miles of former GNSR and HR metals between Aberdeen and Inverness.

There is no coastal area in Britain which has been so devastated by rail closures. The branches to Cruden Bay, where the railway owned a hotel and an electric tramway, and Boddam, to Peterhead, to Fraserburgh and St Combs, to Macduff, to Banff, to Portsoy, Portknockie, Portessie, Buckie and Spey Bay, and to Lossiemouth have all gone. None of the places they served was large, mostly fishing communities, but the railway was much needed and appreciated until the motor rendered it redundant. Even then there were many who wondered if there was not still a place for the railway, but harsh economics and the misfortune of being a long way from the seats of political power did for the GNSR branches. Passenger traffic on the Boddam branch went in 1932, that on the Macduff one in 1951, on the Banff and Lossiemouth branches in 1964, the St Combs and the Fraserburgh in 1965, and the coast line through Portessie and Spey Bay in 1968. Further along the coast, west into Highland Railway territory, the Hopeman branch fared no better, being closed by the LMS as early as 1931.

Lossiemouth, the home town of Britain's first Labour Prime Minister, Ramsay MacDonald, and a fishing and seaside town of some 6,000 people, was distinguished in the

1920s and '30s by being the terminus of the longest regular through service in Britain. This was the 'Aberdonian', the famous sleeping car express which left King's Cross at 7.40 in the evening and arrived at its destination, 608½ miles away, at 10.20 the next morning.

Inverness, close to but not quite on the Moray Firth, was the hub of the Highland system and today it is the most northerly important junction and station on the British Rail network, four lines radiating from Inverness to Aberdeen, Perth, Wick and Kyle of Lochalsh. The Far North line was opened in 1874 and runs for 147½ miles, sometimes beside the sea, sometimes heading far inland to avoid estuaries and other natural obstacles, to Georgemas Junction, where the Wick line

continues to the east coast and the Thurso branch to the north. There were once plans to extend the railway to Scrabster, terminal of the Orkney Islands ferry, but they did not materialize. Inevitably run at a loss and sometimes threatened with extinction, it is a lifeline in this remote and sparsely populated part of the British Isles. There used to be branches to Fortrose, closed in 1951, to Dornoch (worked into BR days by Highland 0-4-4Ts and then by GWR-design pannier tanks hundreds of miles from home until the line's closure in 1960) and from Wick to Lybster, closed in 1944.

As on the GNSR, only one Highland Railway locomotive has survived into preservation. This is No 103 of 1894, long known as the 'Jones Goods', the very first 4-6-0 to run in the British Isles. There were 15 of these long-lived locomotives and they were followed by various classes of this wheel arrangement which monopolized traffic over much of the Highland network until the end of steam. The last CME of the Highland Railway, Christopher Cumming, produced two 4-6-0 designs, the 'Clans' and their smaller-wheeled sisters, originally known as the 'Superheater Goods' but much more familiar in latter days as the 'Clan Goods', and many of these lasted into British Railways days. Finally there were the LMS Stanier '5MTs' which were introduced in 1934 and saw out steam, being replaced by the Class '24', '26' and '27' diesel-electrics in the late 1950s. Nowadays, Class '37' diesel-electrics, equipped with radio signalling, work the Far North line.

WESTERN SCOTLAND

Roads to the Isles

The Kyle of Lochalsh branch leaves the Wick line at Dingwall and heads west through the Highlands amongst scenery that is more spectacular than that of the Far North route, or indeed of practically any route in the British Isles, and then along the shores of Loch Carron to its terminus. Three trains run in each direction all the year round, covering the 82 miles in just under three hours; there are 13 intermediate stations. From Kyle, ferries sail to Skye and the Outer Hebrides, but despite its strategic importance — in steam days it had an engine shed, a sub-depot of Inverness

— it is a very small town, for it has a population of less than 1,000. The Kyle line was a particular haunt of the Cumming 4–6–0s and it was not until the Stainer Class '5s' were permitted on it in the early 1950s that the last 'Clan Goods', No 57954, was withdrawn in October 1952.

Moving south along the deeply indented, beautiful west coast of Scotland, the next line is that to Mallaig, a fishing port at the end of the Road to the Isles from Fort William and

A Class '37' at Fort William with the sleeper train from King's Cross in July 1985.

A Class '37' setting off from Oban with the afternoon train to Dalmally, October 1988.

terminus of the Skye and other Western Isles ferries. The Mallaig line was built by the North British Railway, and leaves Glasgow by the north bank of the Clyde, heads along the shores of Loch Long and Loch Lomond to Crianlarich where it connected with the Caledonian's Oban line, continues north, crosses the remote Rannoch Moor, swings west and so arrives at Fort William. Although this is a terminus station it is not the end of the line, for Mallaig trains reverse out and continue for another 44 miles to their destination. Fort William on Loch Linnhe is a port and a tourist centre and still retains a locomotive depot where the 'K1', 'K4' and the Stanier '5MTs' which have worked holiday specials in recent years are serviced alongside diesels. Fort William was provided with a new station, combined with the tourist centre, a few years back.

The Oban line nowadays shares the same route as that to Fort William out of Glasgow as far as Crianlarich. On both the more powerful Class '37' diesels have ousted the Class '24s', '25s', '26s' and '27s'. In Caledonian and LMS days, the Oban line followed a roundabout route from Glasgow through Stirling, Dunblane and Callander, but British Railways closed this and thus today the Oban route is part North British, part Caledonian. Oban itself is the largest and most developed — but not excessively so — of the West

Highland coastal resorts and towns, full of handsome Victorian and Edwardian hotels, villas and boarding houses in pinky-brown stone bearing names such as 'Balmoral', 'Columba', 'Great Western' and 'Oban Sesame'. The luxuriant gardens reveal that, despite being so far north, down here at sea level winters can often be surprisingly mild regardless of the severity of conditions on the inland heights a few miles away. The station is beside the harbour and the seamen's home, and must be one of the very few in the British Isles where one can look from a carriage window at seals diving for fish thrown from just-docked fishing boats.

The Caledonian Railway designed two classes of 4–6–0 especially for the Oban line. First came McIntosh's '55' Class of 1902–5, a quite small but effective machine known as the 'Oban Bogie', which worked the line until 1937. In the last year of the Caledonian's existence, Pickersgill brought out his outside-cylinder '191' Class. This was better than most of his other 4–6–0s, but nevertheless the class had vanished by the end of the Second World War.

Trains head due south out of Oban, curve north-westwards around the back of the town and reach the waterside again at Connel

Former Caledonian Railway 0–4–4T No 55212 at Ballachulish with the 11.40 to Connel Ferry, 22 August 1948. (*Author's collection*)

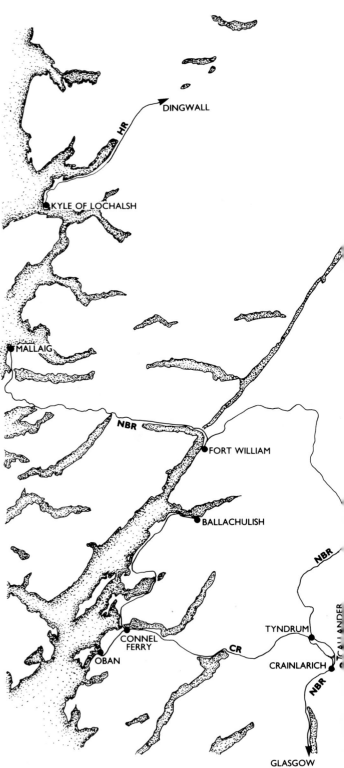

Ferry where there used to be a branch to Ballachulish. They then run within sight of Loch Etive, stop at the sadly derelict although still brightly blue and white painted Taynuilt station and then find themselves running through the lovely Pass of Brander where salmon leap in the river and a series of LNER-built semaphore signals give warnings of possible rock falls. The River Awe opens out into Loch Awe, a green and cream camping coach sits at the disused Loch Awe station whilst across the water a fairy-tale castle completes a picture which epitomizes the delights of rail travel through the Scottish Highlands. For much of its 101½ miles, the Oban to Glasgow line is within sight of water and the final part of its journey brings it down to the resort of Helensburgh whence it runs along the Clyde to its destination.

The Clyde Coast

Competition between the operators of steamship and railway companies was fierce along many estuaries and around several shores in the British Isles, but nowhere could it equal that on the Clyde Coast. There is a saying that 'Glasgow made the Clyde and the Clyde made Glasgow', and the history of the river and the great city through which it flows are inextricably linked.

The world's first successful steamboat, the *Comet*, was launched on the Clyde in 1812. Designed by Henry Bell, who lived in the fashionable resort of Helensburgh some 20 miles down river from Glasgow city centre, the *Comet* began a regular service between the city and the resort. So successful was this that, to quote Ian McCrorie in his *Clyde Pleasure Steamers*, 'Within ten years almost fifty steamboats had been built and engined for the river traffic'. Crowds flocked from the booming, smoke-engulfed, tenement-packed city to Rothesay, Wemyss Bay, Dunoon, Largs and the like. Fifteen years into the century, at the time of Waterloo, these were quiet fishing villages, but 20 or so years further on when Queen Victoria ascended the throne their transformation into great pleasure resorts was almost complete.

Naturally enough, railway companies saw no reason why the shipping lines should monopolize so lucrative a business. Industrial wagonways had existed for nearly a century around Glasgow but no passengers were carried on any of them until the first public railway in Scotland, from Kilmarnock to the coastal town of Troon, was opened in 1817. Horses were, of course, the motive power and the whole affair was pretty primitive, being strictly speaking a plateway rather than a railway proper, but it may nevertheless claim to be the beginning of it all. Steam locomotives appeared in 1831 on the Monkland and Kirkintilloch colliery line, two engines being built by Murdoch, Aitken and Co of Glasgow. Six years later parliamentary authorization was given for the first seaside steam railway proper on the Clyde coast. This

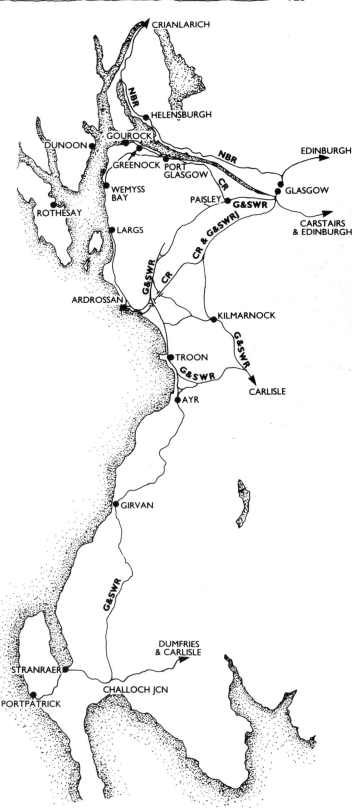

WESTERN SCOTLAND

LMS THE FIRTH OF CLYDE

BY NORMAN WILKINSON. R.I.

A 1925 Norman Wilkinson poster for the LMS.

was the Glasgow, Paisley & Greenock.

It cannot be claimed that the Glasgow, Paisley & Greenock was primarily a line for holidaymakers for Paisley was a world-famous cotton-weaving and fabric-making centre whilst Greenock was a shipbuilding town, so clearly much of the line's profits was expected to come from industry. That said, it is nevertheless true that the company hoped for substantial seaside traffic and on the opening of the line in February 1841 it immediately advertised connections with steamboats — it was actually part owner of two.

The arrival of the railway at Greenock caused a fearful kerfuffle amongst the steamer owners. There was no way they could compete with the railway for speed, so they employed the time-honoured weapon resorted to in such competitive situations — they cut their fares until one could travel the 25 miles from Glasgow to Greenock for 6d (2½p).

As it happened there was enough business for everyone. Glasgow was growing daily. While some of its buildings, its public ones, were — and are — amongst the most magnificent in Britain, its tenements were amongst the most hellish and their inhabitants poured out of them whenever the opportunity offered. These were not as frequent as they ought to have been, for jollification of any sort on Sundays was greatly frowned upon by the Presbyterians, but although they tried

Above Two former G&SWR 'Baltic' tanks and a 4–4–0 at Glasgow St Enoch in 1927. (*H.C. Casserley*)

Right A Caledonian Railway Wemyss Bay 'Pacific' tank at Glasgow Central in original condition, *circa* 1912. (*Author's collection*)

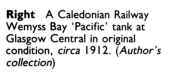

hard they could not stop the boats and trains running on the Sabbath. No doubt there were directors whose conscience and business acumen fought desperate battles — the latter usually won.

The first Glasgow terminus for the Greenock trains was at Bridge Street, immediately south of the river and beside the boat terminal. Later the boats moved across the river nearer to the centre at Broomielaw, then the trains did likewise. The Glasgow, Paisley & Greenock later became part of the Caledonian Railway which opened the magnificent and most aptly named Central station.

The Greenock line was later extended in 1889 three miles westwards through a fiendishly expensive rock tunnel to Gourock,

Left A Gourock to Glasgow Central EMU at Port Glasgow in October 1988.

Below Wemyss Bay station in October 1988.

bringing Dunoon within a 20-minute ferry journey. A pier was erected upon which a substantial station was built and a fast run behind one of the speedy Caledonian 4–4–0s meant that it was possible to travel from Dunoon to the centre of Glasgow in not much over the hour. In 1865 a new branch 10 miles long was opened from the Greenock line at Port Glasgow which climbed inland through the hills and then descended to the sea at Wemyss Bay. A truly splendid station was opened by the Caledonian Railway, all delicate ironwork, glass and panelled wood with a curving, covered walkway leading to the pier. From here steamers left for Rothesay on the Isle of Bute; the journey time to Glasgow was halved, the train and steamer combining to take something less than 1½ hours to this most popular and picturesque of Clyde coast resorts. During the First World War, when holiday traffic on the Clyde was not greatly restricted, the North British Locomotive Co built 12 handsome 'Pacific' tanks especially to handle the traffic over the steeply-graded single branch; although officially classified by the Caledonian as the '944s', they rapidly became known as the Wemyss Bay tanks.

The North British Railway reached Helensburgh on the north bank of the Clyde in 1865, and the pattern was set; the North British had the north bank of the Clyde and the Caledonian had the south, whilst the Ayrshire coast belonged to the Glasgow & South Western. It was not quite as clear cut as this, for the Caledonian competed with the North British out as far as Dumbarton, the G&SWR had a station at Port Glasgow and a very impressive one at Princes Pier, Greenock, whilst the Caledonian retaliated by flinging off a branch deep into Sou' Western territory at Ardrossan. Nevertheless it is interesting to note that when retraction came after the Second World War and lines began to go, it was the incursions which disappeared.

Largs, south of Wemyss Bay, was reached by a rather roundabout G&SWR line from Glasgow in 1885, trains heading south-west from Paisley to Ardrossan and then back up the coast almost due north.

One of the truly great railway writers was David L. Smith. He died recently but he left behind some marvellous pieces on his favourite line, the Sou'-West. In the *Railway Annual* of 1949 he described the arrival of a 'packed train of sixteen coaches' on Paisley Fair Saturday at Largs. The line was newly opened, Davie, the fireman, had been there once before but the driver, McConnachie, never. This is what happened. 'They came swiftly round the curve in the cutting, and there was the terminus ahead of them. "Is that the station?" enquired Davie. "Aye," said McConnachie. "Weel," cried Davie, straining furiously at his already tight tender hand-brake, "we're no' gaun t' stoap!" Six bright Largs youths sat like crows on the buffers until about ten seconds before the engine struck. Eight of the alighting passengers were injured, but none seriously. The guard never braked at all.' Observing an EMU glide silently out of Largs the Saturday before I re-read the above account, I reflected there was a lot to be said for modern technology and well-trained crews, even if it results in a certain lack of drama.

South from Ardrossan the coast line continued through Troon, past its famous golf course and on to Ayr.

Another of David L. Smith's most extraordinary stories concerns another Fair Saturday, this time a Glasgow one. When the fare-paying patrons had been sent safely home it was the custom of most of the railway staff at Ayr to go down in the otherwise empty carriages to Girvan and return after a hard evening's drinking early on the Sunday morning. On this particular occasion the engine ran out of steam on a bank outside Ayr, the crew put on the blower and, whilst waiting, fell asleep. Next thing they knew it was broad daylight, the fire was out, and not a soul was stirring in the train. Driver and fireman gathered some sticks from a wood alongside the track, got the fire going, raised steam and 'pulled into Ayr when the folks were just getting up to begin their Sabbath round'. As for the passengers, 'they never heard a word about it'.

WESTERN SCOTLAND

Ayr is a town with a long history, and it was a port long before anyone had ever thought of railways. In 1840 the Glasgow, Paisley, Kilmarnock & Ayr Railway had opened, and the industry inland towards Kilmarnock provided the company's successor, the G&SWR, with lucrative business. Ayr became a favoured resort and a complex series of lines fed into its busy station. Southwards boat trains from Glasgow to Stranraer continued to Girvan on the coast and then turned inland heading due south until they reached Challoch Junction. Here they met up with the line from Carlisle and Dumfries whence they did a 90 degree turn and so reached their destination.

The changed social conditions of the post-Second World War world opened new horizons for many Glaswegians as it did for

Left A former Clyde Coast 'blue train' EMU at Helensburgh station in October 1988.

Below A mural painted by students of Largs Academy at Largs station, October 1988.

so many other citizens of the British Isles, but affluence and the motor car dealt harshly with the Clyde resorts. The boats which had once raced up and down the river, three or four sometimes tieing up alongside, now found fewer and fewer customers and were gradually taken out of service and broken up, although the last of the Clyde paddle-steamers, the *Waverley*, built for the LNER in 1947, has been successfully preserved. There was still business for the ferries, from Gourock to Dunoon and Wemyss Bay to Rothesay for example, but even these had to carry cars to survive.

In the heyday of competition the three railway companies had on occasions used their heaviest and fastest express engines, although these were often quite unsuited to the short distances involved. Fast acceleration rather than high top speeds was what was needed and such classes as the high-stepping

A Stanier Class '5MT' with an inspection saloon passing a 'Crab' 2–6–0 and a Class '26' at Falkland Junction, Ayr, on 20 July 1966. (*C.J.M. Lofthus*)

North British 'Atlantics' were vastly out of place; tank engines of the same wheel arrangement were, however, ideal, and the NBR 4-4-2Ts were a familiar sight on the Helensburgh line for some 40 years. The Caledonian used everything from 4-6-0s and 4-4-0s to 0-6-0s and 0-4-4Ts as well, of course, as Pickersgill's especially designed Wemyss Bay tanks. The Glasgow & South Western favoured similar wheel arrangements but went one better in its last year of existence and brought out the heaviest locomotives yet seen in Scotland, the 99-ton 4-6-4Ts. Their designer, Robert Whitelegg, based them on the 4-6-4Ts he had built for another seaside line, the London, Tilbury & Southend. A Sou' West 'Baltic' in full flight on an Ayrshire coast train was one of the most awesome spectacles ever seen on rails.

After 1923, LMS 4-4-0s and then 2-6-4Ts of both LMS and BR Standard design and BR 4-6-0s took over most of the southside Clyde Coast workings whilst Gresley 2-6-2Ts slowly ousted the North British 4-4-0s and 4-4-2Ts. In 1953 W.A.C. Smith wrote: 'The

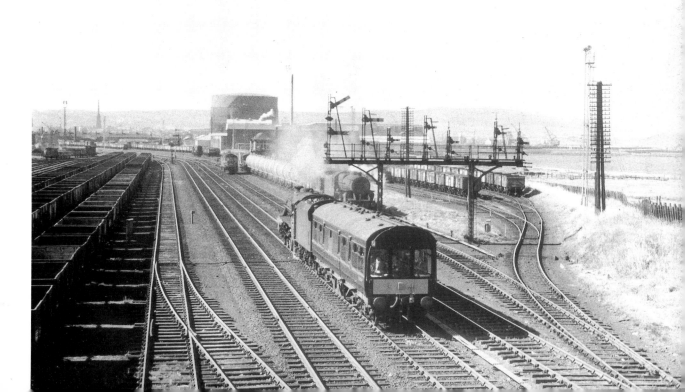

Clyde Coast services have come under severe criticism from both residents and visitors, for the present service can stand no comparison even with that of 1939, and still less with that of the highly competitive days'. However, this was to be their lowest ebb for electrification would bring about a lasting revival.

The first sections to be so treated covered former North British territory north of the Clyde, some 52 route miles from Airdrie in the east, through Glasgow Queen Street Low Level and along the river to Helensburgh. The 50 cycle ac overhead system was chosen, working at 25kV except in the central underground sections where it was reduced to 6.25kV. The trains which British Railways ordered were in advance of anything they had yet provided for suburban travel, and painted in what was for those days a startling livery of Caledonian blue they had streamlined cab fronts with wrap-round windows, air-operated sliding doors and a saloon layout. They were fitted with Gresley bogies and rode very well. Unfortunately problems were soon experienced and for a while steam had to come back, but eventually the Blue Trains, as they quickly became known, established themselves as firm favourites with the Glaswegian travelling public.

Electrification reached the southern Clyde resorts in 1967 when steam was banished from the Gourock and Wemyss Bay lines in September of that year. Further Blue Trains came into service, bringing the total of three-car units, of classes '303' and '311', to 110. Next was the turn of the Largs and Ardrossan services, in 1979. For these, 16 units of a new type, the '314s', were built. Similar in appearance to units at work out of King's Cross and on Merseyside, they do not have the elegance of the '303s' but are very well appointed internally with toilets and gangway connections within the three-car units. In 1987 electrification reached down the coast to Ayr, and updated versions of the '314s', the '318s', were provided for this scheme. In practice, the various types of Glasgow area EMUs tend to wander all over the system,

and nowadays wear the black and orange Strathclyde livery. They are kept commendably clean and in my experience are quite bereft of graffiti, which says something about both Glaswegians and the railway authorities.

There are a surprising number of handsome well-looked-after nineteenth century stations on the Clyde Coast lines, both in the suburban area and further out, although inevitably there are some bus-shelter type horrors dating from the misguided 1960s and '70s. The four-platform Paisley Gilmour Street is very fine and Port Glasgow has much to commend it, as does Greenock Central, whilst a number of the seaside termini are especially distinctive; the beautiful Wemyss Bay is the best of the lot. Gourock was rebuilt and reopened by the Provost in 1987, whilst Largs has a fine modern mural entitled 'A Celebration of the Railway' painted by students of Largs Academy.

The basic weekday frequency of the Largs to Glasgow service is hourly, as is that from Ardrossan Town, which means that Ardrossan South beach, where the two lines join, has a half-hourly service. Ardrossan Harbour still has a station, for the Arran boat; it is reduced to a single, bare platform, but semaphore signals and G&SWR boxes remained intact and operational in 1989. The Glasgow to Ayr trains run every half-hour, Glasgow to Wemyss Bay every hour and those between Gourock and Glasgow Central every 20 minutes approximately. The Helensburgh to Airdrie via Glasgow Queen Street service runs every half-hour.

Although the days of spectacle may be past, when 'Pacific' and 'Baltic' tanks brought transatlantic passengers down to join Cunard and Canadian Pacific liners, or raced each other to the numerous piers where the *Duchess of Hamilton, Glen Sannox* or some other still remembered steamer strained at her hawsers, the fast, regular, clean and comfortable electric trains of today have proved what was by no means certain 25 years ago, that there will always be a demand for train services along the shores of the Clyde.

THE NORTH WEST

Stranraer to Larne

The Carlisle to Stranraer line was opened throughout in 1862. Stranraer is on Loch Ryan and handy enough for Larne, but across the peninsula was Portpatrick which was even nearer to Ireland and the Glasgow & South Western built a joint line to it with the Caledonian. But it was a difficult line to work, Stranraer proved more convenient and although the Portpatrick line did not close until 1950, boat trains to Ireland had long ceased to use it. The Portpatrick & Wigtown Joint Railway also struck south from Newton Stewart through Wigtown to the coast at Garlieston (later Millisle) and Whithorn. Both closed in 1950. Further east along Solway Firth the Castle Douglas to Kirkcudbright branch closed in 1965 at the same time as the entire main line from Dumfries to Challoch Junction.

This, however, did not mean the end of boat trains between Carlisle and Stranraer for they were diverted albeit by a highly roundabout route, but with the benefit of electric power south of the Border the day boat train today takes 8 hours 26 minutes to cover the 465 miles from Euston to Stranraer, compared with 10 hours 38 minutes for the $372\frac{3}{4}$ miles by the direct route in 1947. Stranraer to Larne is the busiest of all the Irish Sea freight routes, but neither Northern Irish Railways nor British Rail has received much government encouragement to carry freight and they have consequently succumbed to the road lobby. On the passenger side there has been

LMS-built Compound 4–4–0 No 916 at Stranraer Harbour with a boat train from Glasgow, 21 June 1937. (*H.C. Casserley*)

rather more enterprise, and when the first moves away from a corporate BR livery began in the early 1980s a rake of Mark 1 corridors employed on the Glasgow-Stranraer boat services appeared in a startling candy stripe ensemble labelled 'Sealink'.

Across the North Channel boat trains have always featured prominently in Larne's schedules, too. The very last ordinary steam-worked passenger services within the British Isles were to be found on rush-hour workings between Belfast and Larne until 1970, in the charge of 'WT' Class 2-6-4Ts.

With the end of steam in Northern Ireland in the early 1970s and the takeover of all passenger workings by diesel multiple units, the Railway Preservation Society of Ireland stepped in and secured a fleet of historic carriages and the steam engines to haul them. That one sentence gives absolutely no indication of the vast undertaking this actually was, the restoration to running order of locomotives and a complete train of vintage stock, all accomplished in or close to Belfast at a time when, if the media was to be believed, the entire city and its environs was embarked on an orgy of destruction. One of the highlights inaugurated at that time, and

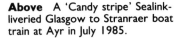

Above A 'Candy stripe' Sealink-liveried Glasgow to Stranraer boat train at Ayr in July 1985.

Left A Class '37' at Stranraer in July 1985.

Above right The Railway Preservation Society of Ireland's Vintage Train at Whitehead Excursion station, headed by former GNR Compound 4-4-0 No 85 *Merlin*, August 1986.

Right The 'Portrush Flier', headed by former NCC 2-6-4T No 4, climbing out of Portrush in August 1977.

repeated every summer since, was a series of runs between Belfast and Portrush, the 'Portrush Flier'. Once again it was possible for enthusiasts and day-trippers to sample the delicious smells of steam coal as they headed out of Belfast towards the equally distinctive aromas of bracing Portrush.

Of all the extraordinary achievements of the preservation movement in Britain and Ireland since the 1960s none surely ranks higher than that of the RPSI. With rather more co-operation from the railway authorities on both sides of the border than English, Welsh and Scottish groups have often received from British Rail, the RPSI has taken its vintage train, steam hauled, the length and breadth of the country. It has its base at Whitehead, at the excursion station built in the early years of the present century beside Belfast Lough on the Belfast (York Road) to Larne line.

Furness and the Lakes

The railway which runs south from Carlisle around the shores of Solway Firth, the Irish

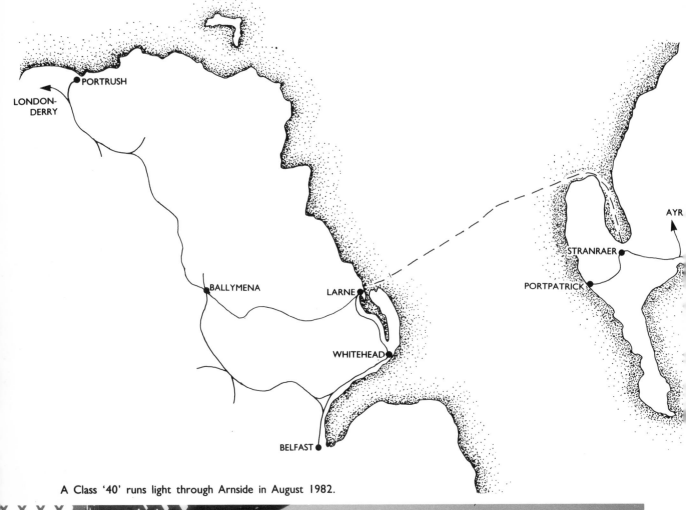

A Class '40' runs light through Arnside in August 1982.

KILMARNOCK &
GLASGOW

GLASGOW

DUMFRIES

KIRTLEBRIDGE

P&WJR

G&SWR

CR

G&SWR

EDINBURGH

SOLWAY VIADUCT

CR

NBR

PORT CARLISLE

CASTLE
DOUGLAS

NBR

WIGTOWN

CARLISLE

NEWCASTLE

SILLOTH

KIRKCUDBRIGHT

M&CR

LEEDS

GARLIESTON

CR

LANCASTER

WHITHORN

ASPATRIA

MARYPORT

LNWR → PENRITH

WORKINGTON

WHITEHAVEN

ST BEES

FR

RAVENGLASS &
ESKDALE RAILWAY

ESKDALE

CONISTON

RAMSEY

RAVENGLASS

MANX
ELECTRIC
RAILWAY

SNAEFELL

PEEL

LAXEY

DOUGLAS

I.O.M. RAILWAY

PORT ERIN

THE NORTH WEST

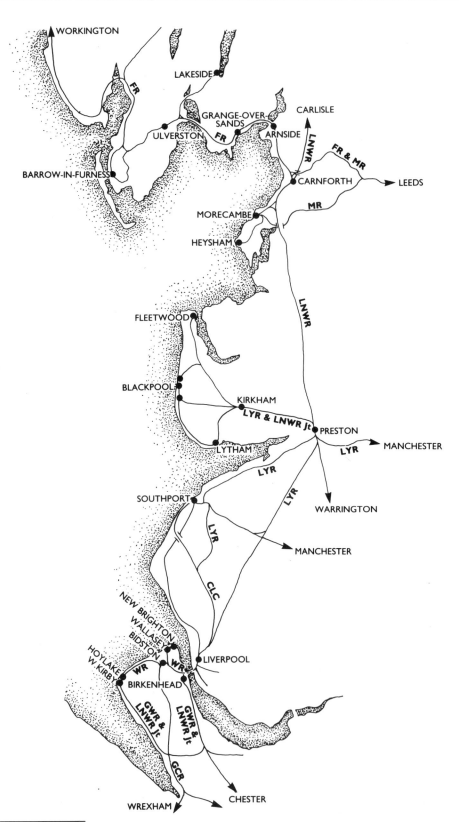

RAILWAYS TO THE COAST

Sea and Morecambe Bay and rejoins the West Coast main line at Carnforth is an excellent example of a line whose route was predetermined by geography. Throughout its 114 miles length it seldom loses sight of the sea, for there is nowhere else it could go; any move inland brings it up against the mountains of the most spectacularly beautiful area of England. There was only one line which ever penetrated the heart of the Lake District and conquered it, linking the sea directly with the West Coast main line, that from Penrith through Keswick to Workington. This served its community faithfully for over 100 years but did not survive the Beeching era.

A glance at the map gives the impression that the coast route from Carnforth to Carlisle is one continuous line. In a sense it is, but it was originally a number of different railways, constructed and owned by several companies, linked to each other, though not always totally amicably. Even today the British Rail timetable shows it as two sections, from Lancaster to Carnforth and Barrow, and from Barrow to Carlisle. However, many trains actually work right around the coast, and BR quite rightly promotes the line as a scenic route and a leisurely alternative to the direct main line between Lancaster and Carlisle. Steam excursions, the 'Cumbrian Coast Express' principally, are a regular feature.

Full-scale resorts, in the terms of those found further south, such as Morecambe, Blackpool and Southport, do not exist in this part of the world. Nevertheless there are some attractive seaside towns and villages. Maryport and Silloth, on the Solway Firth, are both resorts, and although neither is, nor ever was, very big, they attracted railway speculators early on. The Maryport and Carlisle was a 27½-mile line engineered by George Stephenson. It opened in the spring of 1843 and was part of a through route linking the west coast and George's native east coast by way of the Newcastle upon Tyne & Carlisle Railway, later part of the North Eastern. The idea was that traffic from the Continent would be shipped into Newcastle, taken by train to Maryport and then complete the

journey by sea to Ireland. This ambition was not realized and the Maryport & Carlisle was never of much more than local importance.

It was intended that Silloth should become 'the Torquay of the North', and despite the enraged opposition of the Maryport & Carlisle, which considered that bit of Cumberland its own private preserve, the Carlisle & Silloth Bay Railway and Dock Company was opened in August 1856. As with Maryport, the grandiose plans for Silloth were almost ludicrously over-ambitious. However, the line offered the North British Railway a route into Carlisle and its line from Edinburgh joined the Carlisle & Silloth's on the north-west outskirts of the city at Canal Junction. There was also a branch off the branch to Port Carlisle which is chiefly remembered for the NBR constructing a new, horse-worked tramcar for it as late as 1908! Eventually the nineteenth century caught up with it in the second decade of the twentieth — then the LNER closed the passenger service in 1932. The Silloth branch pursued its own affairs for over 100 years and was closed in the Beeching era in September 1964.

The Caledonian Railway could not bear to let its great rival the NBR appropriate a little bit of England unchallenged, so it built a line from Kirtlebridge, on the West Coast Main Line between Gretna and Lockerbie, to the NBR Silloth line, over which it obtained running powers as far as Abbey Town, then continued on to link up with the Maryport & Carlisle north-east of Aspatria.

We have noted the Workington to Penrith line, the only one which ran from the Cumbrian coast line right through the Lake District to link up with the LNWR's Anglo-Scottish main line, but there were a number of freight lines which penetrated some way inland from Workington and Whitehaven, and three passenger carrying lines further south in Furness Railway territory.

It is not an area into which holidaymakers came from any distance, looking for beaches and all the usual seaside attractions. The three largest towns served by the line, Barrow-in-Furness, Whitehaven and Work-

A Carlisle to Barrow-in-Furness DMU approaching Whitehaven in April 1985.

ington, are all purely industrial centres, each with its harbour. Workington has a shingle beach, St Bees, the next station to the south of Whitehaven, has sands from which it is safe to bathe, and there are many other undeveloped beaches all along the coast, although often currents and the fear of nuclear contamination make them dangerous for swimmers. Workington was a steel town and steel meant much business for the railway. When the works were closed down in 1981, unemployment in Workington went up from just under 10 per cent to over 22 per cent. Few families were unaffected, and railwaymen were amongst those who lost their jobs.

Like the town itself there was nothing glamorous about the engines which lived at Workington; in early 1956 the 27 shedded there were made up of six standard Fowler 0-6-0T shunting engines, seven standard Fowler '4F' 0-6-0s, six of their successors, the Ivatt 0-6-0s, seven of their little brother '2MTs', one Fowler '2P' passenger 4-4-0, and one of the last five surviving Furness Railway 0-6-0s, No 52499. Named locomotives came later, in the diesel era, for the pioneer Class '40s' were a familiar sight on steel trains for over 20 years and they were

still to be found there when they had long vanished from other, once familiar, territories.

The Coniston branch of the Furness Railway opened in June 1859 and closed in 1958. The others are still working, at least in part. A very similar line to the Coniston branch, that to Lakeside on the most famous of all the lakes, Windermere, was opened from the Furness main line at Plumpton Junction, near Ulverston, in June 1869. Ulverston, the 'capital of Furness', was once a port, being linked to the sea by what has been described as the 'shortest, straightest, deepest and widest canal in Britain'. At its height some 300 vessels regularly worked around the coast from Ulverston but the canal ceased to be used around the time of the First World War. The Furness Railway built a particularly fine station and its splendid brickwork, iron railings, awnings and lamps survive and have recently been restored.

The branch line trains from Ulverston connected at Lakeside with a fleet of Barrow-built steamers, owned from 1872 by the Furness Railway, which sailed to various other spots on the lake shore, and the visitors came pouring in, the traffic reaching its zenith in the Edwardian era. It was not quite the seaside, although trains ran around the edge of Morecambe Bay, over the estuary at Arnside, and along the sea wall at Grange to reach the

Crossing Arnside Viaduct — the view from a DMU, April 1987.

branch. The Windermere steamers had the great advantage over ocean-going ones that their intrepid passengers ran no risk of sea-sickness, and for many it was quite as near a sea voyage as they had any wish to get.

The line did plenty of business in the holi-day season but less and less out of it, and from 1938 onwards winter passenger services ceased. German prisoners of war provided unexpected patronage during the Second World War, then the holidaymakers came back in 1946 but by the 1960s their numbers had fallen below a level considered economic and so passenger services came to an end in September 1965; goods traffic lasted a further two years until the ironworks at Backbarrow, near Haverthwaite, closed.

A Furness Railway 4–6–4T and a 2–4–0 meet on Arnside Viaduct in about 1920. (*K.J. Norman collection*)

Above The Lakeside terminus of the Lakeside & Haverthwaite Railway in May 1986.

Left The Eskdale terminus of the Ravenglass & Eskdale Railway, April 1986.

But this was not the end, for moves were afoot to preserve the line. It was originally hoped to retain the entire branch and a number of steam locomotives were stored at Carnforth depot for use on it. In the event only the northernmost section from Haverthwaite to the lake was reopened, on 2 May 1973.

The other steam railway in Cumbria is the Ravenglass & Eskdale. It began in May 1875 as a 3-foot gauge mineral line running for seven miles from mines in Eskdale down the valley to a connection with the Furness Railway on the coast. Passengers were carried but neither they nor the mines could keep the line solvent and after years of struggle it gave up in the spring of 1913. Its saviour was the remarkable model engineer W.J. Bassett-Lowke. He needed a testing ground for his 15-inch gauge locomotives and decided to take over the R&ER and convert it to that gauge. This he did and reopened virtually all of it in 1916. After varying fortunes, in 1960

the line looked like closing for good, but it was once again saved, this time by the efforts of local people and steam enthusiasts all over the country.

Since then it has greatly prospered, attracting many of the ever-increasing number of visitors who come to the Lake District each year. New engines have appeared, including *Northern Rock*, a 2–6–2 described as 'probably the most powerful 15-inch gauge engine in the world', which was built in the railway's workshops at Ravenglass in 1976. The BR station building there was taken over when it became an unstaffed halt (it was converted into a public house, the Ratty Arms) and the first radio controlled trains in Britain began in 1977. The views all along the line are amongst the finest on any stretch of railway, ranging from those of the sea, the estuary of the River Mite and the towers of Windscale atomic power station, to waterfalls and the great Lake District pikes and fells, including Scafell Pike, the highest mountain in England.

Barrow-in-Furness itself is a sombre town with a magnificent late Victorian town hall and a modern station rebuilt after the Furness Railway one was destroyed by bombs in the Second World War, is still almost totally dependent on shipbuilding. It is not much more than an hour away from Morecambe by train and for a time was also linked to it by steamer.

At the Carnforth end of the line, Arnside and Grange-over-Sands stations are right beside the sea. Arnside is a fairly basic station, although it has a nice iron footbridge and a neat little brick building on the up platform which now belongs to the Arnside/Silverdale AONB Countryside Management Service. Immediately beyond Arnside is the famous viaduct much beloved of photographers which allows the railway to cut across Morecambe Bay in a far more direct line than the road and head straight for Grange-over-Sands.

The Furness Railway went to some lengths to develop Grange-over-Sands as a resort at the end of the last century and the railway

skirts the coast in a manner reminiscent of the sea wall at Dawlish. Grange did grow quite considerably and although it never became a resort in the true sense — for Grange-over-Mud might be a more accurate description and bathing is not really possible — nevertheless it is a rather beautiful place. Handsome villas set amongst luxuriant trees and shrubbery overlooking the bay remind one of Killiney on Dublin Bay or even the French Riviera. Grange is the sort of place where one finds public conveniences rather than lavatories; there are tea rooms and gentlemen's outfitters, tennis courts and a delightful station carefully looked after and scarcely changed since Victorian times.

A modern poster for the Isle of Man, where coastal railways and trams are still very much a part of modern holiday attractions.

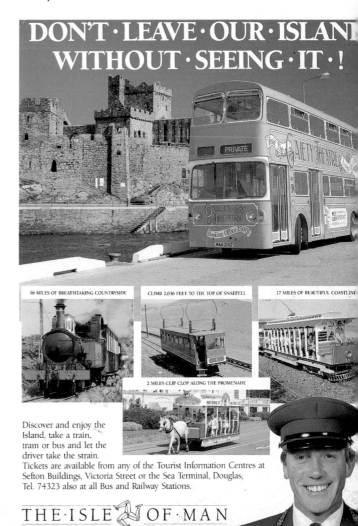

The Isle of Man

Opposite Furness, and visible from it on a clear day, is the Isle of Man. In the nineteenth century the island developed into one of the most popular destinations for holidaymakers from Northern England, North Wales, Ireland and Scotland. Indeed the summit of the island's highest mountain, Snaefell, is the only spot in the British Isles from which, on a clear day, every country which makes up the British Isles can be seen.

Without an extensive transport system the island would never have attracted visitors on the scale it did. An electric tramway was built to the summit of Snaefell in 1895. It ran from the coast at Laxey where it connected with the Manx Electric Railway, opened two years earlier. This eventually extended $17\frac{1}{2}$ miles along the eastern coast of the island between the two principal towns, Ramsey and Douglas.

Pioneer though the island was in electric railways, it was the steam engine which opened it up to the visitors. In 1873 the first $11\frac{1}{2}$ miles opened of a system which, at its zenith, would see the departure from Douglas, the island's principal station and 'the biggest and best narrow gauge station in Britain', of over 100 trains each day.

The Beyer Peacock 3-foot gauge 2-4-0Ts (based on a design for the Norwegian State Railways but also relatives of the London Underground 4-4-0Ts, 15 of which were built between 1873 and 1926) became, and remain, justly famous. They hauled trains along the south-east coast from Port Erin, through Castletown to Douglas, from there across the island to the west coast at Peel, then up the west coast before swinging eastwards to Ramsey.

Although both steam and electric railways

Victoria Pier, Douglas, Isle of Man, *circa* 1913. (*Author's collection*)

VICTORIA PIER, DOUGLAS, I. O. M.

began to suffer road competition in the 1930s, the entire narrow gauge network remained intact in 1939. For a short while after 1945 the good times returned, but soon the competition began to bite. In November 1965 services were suspended, and did not start up again for the 1966 season. There was a brief revival in 1967 but a year later the Peel and Ramsey lines were shut for good. Eventually all the surviving lines, steam and electric, passed into Isle of Man Government control.

In the 1970s the future of any form of rail transport in the island seemed problematical, but the realization that it possessed a unique Victorian museum of working transport encouraged the Isle of Man government to invest in and publicize the steam and electric systems. Under the control of the Department of Tourism and Transport, four steam locomotives, built between 1874 and 1910, and a fleet of vintage carriages and tramcars, the oldest of which, Manx Electric Railway cars Nos 1 and 2, dating from 1893, are said to be the oldest working trams in regular use in the world, now attract not only enthusiasts but lots of ordinary holidaymakers in search of something different. In addition there is the restored 2-foot gauge Groundle Glen Railway, where the Bagnall engine *Sea Lion* of 1896 takes visitors down to Sea Lion Cove, whilst the Douglas Horse Tramway operates along the promenade of the island's premier town, as it has since 1876.

Morecambe

One doesn't normally associate the Midland Railway with the seaside, but one of the most popular resorts in the country owes both its existence and its name to it. Well, almost.

Excursion trains in the charge of Stanier '5MT' 4–6–0s at Morecambe (LNWR), *circa* 1958.

Strictly speaking it was the North Western Railway, often known as the little North Western to avoid confusion with the LNWR, which opened a railway from Lancaster to a proposed port on Morecambe Bay close to Poulton-le-Sands in June 1848. Although independent it was very much influenced by the Midland, was worked by it from the summer of 1852 and was absorbed by it in June 1871.

Poulton-le-Sands was already something of a small resort and the suggested port and part of a scheme which included a canal and would provide a new approach to the wharves alongside the River Lune at Lancaster. The only part of the scheme which came into existence was the harbour at Morecambe, as it gradually came to be known, although the station was originally called Poulton. Morecambe was not much of a harbour and although steamers sailed from it across the bay to Barrow and to Northern Ireland it soon lost the latter traffic, first to Barrow, and then, at the beginning of the present century, to Heysham. However, Morecambe bore the loss with equanimity for it developed ambitions in another direction. The railway built the North Western Hotel in 1848 and the

holidaymakers began to pour in.

Morecambe is, of course, in Lancashire, but it is not far from the Yorkshire border and by June 1850 the Midland and the little North Western Railways had jointly completed a through route from Leeds and Bradford by way of Keighley, Skipton, Wennington and Lancaster. Morecambe rapidly became extremely popular, even if its beaches were a bit muddy at low tide, and its proximity to the lakes and mountains gave it an advantage over its two great rivals further down the coast, Blackpool and Southport. Businessmen took up residence and the 'Leeds, Bradford and Morecambe Working Man's Residential Express' was, by the early 1900s, covering the journey in under two hours. In the early days there was a direct service between King's Cross and Morecambe, when MR trains used the GNR terminus before the building of St Pancras.

Meanwhile, the LNWR quite reasonably considered Morecambe to be within its territory and saw no reason why the Midland Railway should cream off all its traffic, so it built a short branch from the West Coast main line at Hest Bank in 1864. The junction

Visitors Arriving at Morecambe.

Below left A Leeds train leaving the former Midland Railway station at Morecambe on Spring Bank Holiday Monday, 1987.

Right A postcard from Edwardian Morecambe, LNWR.

faced north, which was not very convenient as most traffic came from Lancaster and the south, but it was 22 years before a south curve was opened. Truth to tell, the LNWR was never very quick on the uptake when it came to realizing the potential of seaside resorts. For example, the Lancashire & Yorkshire was much the senior partner at Blackpool, the only LNWR trains into Southport were carriages detached from Euston to Liverpool trains at Edge Hill, the Cheshire Lines Committee shared New Brighton with the Wirral, and the Midland Railway got in first at Morecambe.

Both the LNWR and the Midland replaced their original Morecambe stations, the former with the appropriately named Euston Road in 1888, the latter with the equally appropriate Promenade, facing the sea, the ponies and the preachers urging the masses to 'Store up treasure in Heaven', in 1907.

Morecambe harbour, as we have seen, was a poor thing and the Midland Railway decided that if it was going to provide any sort of challenge to the GWR, the LNWR, the Furness and the Glasgow & South Western for the Irish Sea traffic it was going to have to find itself a decent harbour. Thus Heysham, three miles south down the coast from Morecambe, was opened in September 1904. Steamers began regular sailings to Dublin, Belfast, Londonderry and Douglas, Isle of Man, and boat trains to and from St Pancras became one of the highlights of the passenger service over the 'Little North Western' route.

The Midland invested heavily in Morecambe in the first decade of the present century as the holiday business continued to boom. In addition to the new Promenade station and Heysham Harbour, electric trains, the first to operate over Midland rails, began to run between Lancaster, Morecambe and Heysham in July 1908, the first example of the single-phase ac system in Britain. The service lasted into British Railways days, was replaced by steam in February 1951, and then, most interestingly, was re-electrified some 2½ years later. Modified former LNWR Oerlikon stock, originally built for the Euston suburban services, replaced the Midland Railway trains, and this re-incarnation lasted until the end of 1965.

In the 1930s the LMS built a hotel at Morecambe which is now, with its elegant, sweeping reinforced concrete curves, a real period piece. Competition from motor coaches and cars was a force to be reckoned with by this date and once Morecambe had recovered from wartime and early post-war restrictions, the railway's proportion of the resort's holiday traffic fell rapidly away. Indeed, its decline is such that I have seen Morecambe station completely deserted on a sunny Bank Holiday Monday despite the resort being packed with day-trippers, virtually all of whom must have arrived by car or coach. When a train for Leeds eventually pulled in its three carriages were more than adequate for the numbers which presented themselves at the station.

Today all services, exclusively diesel-powered, are concentrated on the Promenade station which is perfectly placed right beside the fun-fair and just south of the now derelict pier, badly damaged in a storm in November 1977. The station has four platform faces, two with an awning just sufficient for a three-coach train. Between platforms three and four there is a centre road with a rusty crossover to enable long-vanished locomotives to back out of the station. The buildings are handsome, in pale yellow stone with a substantial awning outside, whilst inside there is much stylish Edwardian decorative tiling and two very large lavatories, thoughtfully provided by the Midland railway since many of its excursion trains were made up of non-corridor, non-lavatory stock. The station has a slightly neglected air but essentially is in good repair and is a fine example of early twentieth-century railway architecture. Where once the electric trains ran, a DMU shuttle operates some 25 journeys each weekday (around ten on Sundays) between Lancaster and Morecambe, taking 10–11 minutes for the four-mile journey with a stop at Bare Lane on the outskirts of Morecambe.

The Belfast boat trains between Leeds and Heysham provided the 'Jubilee' Class 4–6–0s with some of their last top link duties in 1966, but these trains are now a thing of the past for the last Heysham to Belfast boat sailed in April 1975. The direct Midland main line from Wennington through Hornby and Lancaster Green Ayre to Heysham and Morecambe closed in 1966, but a fairly basic service still operates from Yorkshire by way of Carnforth. However, there is no provision, not even on summer Saturdays, for extra holiday traffic, all trains stopping at virtually all stations.

Heysham is still served by a limited number of freight trains, chiefly for the nuclear power station. The passenger station, forming part of the ferry terminal buildings, had a deserted air for many years in the late 1970s and the 1980s, while Heysham itself went into a decline in the early 1970s when traffic dropped away, not least that to Belfast.

The Northern Irish troubles contributed to this sad state of affairs, culminating in the end of the Sealink Northern Irish sailings in April 1975; Isle of Man services had finished the previous year.

However, better times were on their way and in 1978 the Isle of Man service was reinstated and, although passenger trains no longer ran into Heysham Harbour, the Isle of Man Steam Packet Seaways advertised rail connections to and from Lancaster, a coach providing the link. This was better than nothing, but there was great rejoicing when for the summer of 1988 a through boat train was once again advertised to Heysham. It started from Stockport and travelling by way of Manchester, Bolton and Morecambe, reaching Heysham harbour in 2 hours 10 minutes. It is a welcome revival, though nothing so grand as the 'Residential Express' of days gone by.

Biggest and best

What can one say of Blackpool which will do it justice? We can begin with a statement of fact which is that it is Britain's premier resort. Neither as toffee-nosed as Bournemouth, nor as cosmopolitan as Brighton, not as elegant as Torquay, not as bracing as Scarborough, not as scenic as the Clyde Coast resorts nor as spectacular as Llandudno, it nevertheless outstrips them all in the visitors it attracts. And nowhere is there a resort which owes more to the railways for its success.

The first train steamed into Blackpool on 29 April 1846. This was not really the beginning, however; excursionists had been arriving for some six years previously, since the Preston & Wyre Railway had been opened, linking the manufacturing town with Fleetwood on the Wyre estuary. The P&W's Poulton station was only a half-hour cart ride away from Blackpool, and there were plenty who made the journey, to the hotels, the boarding houses and the sands. Fleetwood

Blackpool Central in about 1912.
(*Author's collection*)

was the creation of Sir Peter Hesketh Fleetwood, a member of a still well-known Lancashire family. Planned as a port and a resort, if Sir Peter's intentions had been fulfilled the Blackpool with which we are all so familiar might never have come about. But they weren't. Although Fleetwood was for a short time on the direct west coast route between London and Glasgow, boats linking its railhead with Ardrossan, it did not develop as its creator had hoped and its failure almost bankrupted him.

As Blackpool continued to outstrip Fleetwood in popularity it became obvious that it would need its own railway, so a branch was opened from Poulton to a quite impressive-looking station at Talbot Road at the north end of the town. As early as 1 June 1849, five trains headed towards Blackpool from various east Lancashire mill towns. By the time they had reached Bolton and were heading, one after the other, westwards, they had on board something over 10,000 passengers, crammed into 198 carriages and wagons. So numerous were the excursionists that they had to be divided up between Fleetwood and Blackpool, for neither resort could accommodate such a number.

What was the peculiar attraction of Blackpool? Well, to begin with it was in the right place. The railways made it possible for each of the hundreds of thousands of mill-workers and mine-workers and their families living in the expanding, teeming towns of Lancashire to travel to Blackpool, spend a whole day there, and be home again that evening. And what did all these people do when they got to Blackpool? They walked along its fine sands and bathed in its safe waters. That was certainly enough in the early days. Other resorts, notably Morecambe and Southport, could offer much the same and they, of course, attracted vast numbers of visitors too. But what made Blackpool pre-eminent was the enterprise of a number of its citizens and its Corporation. This latter came into being in 1876, at a time when the economy of the country was in decline, affecting Blackpool, as it did everywhere else. The number of visitors fell by over a third in one year and continued to fall. Something had to be done — and it was.

At the considerable cost of £3,500 the Corporation installed the first proper street lighting system in the kingdom. It was inaugurated on the evening of 19 September 1879 and it was estimated that around 100,000 came to see the brilliant Siemens arc lights spring to life; most, naturally, arrived by train. The event was really the beginning of what is still probably Blackpool's biggest attraction, the Illuminations. The town never looked back.

Having installed the electric light,

Blackpool then decided it must have an electric tramway. Once again it beat everyone else to it. Other-towns had horse or cable or even steam-propelled tramways, and some had tentative plans to electrify them. But when the first Blackpool electric tram ceremoniously set out along the promenade on 29 September 1885 it was the beginning of street tramways in these islands. The Glasgow system, the largest in Scotland, would not have its first electric route until 1898, and the greatest of them all, London, did not begin regular operation of electric trams until 1901. And whilst all that remains of these, and all the many systems, large and small, which reached their zenith around 1914, is to be found in museums, the 104-year-long career of the Blackpool tramway is unbroken and looks certain to extend far into the next cen-

Left A Class '47' pulls out of Blackpool North with a Nottingham express in May 1988.

Below Blackpool promenade in August 1982 with 1979-built tram No 761 approaching.

tury. However, there was a time not so very long ago when its survival was under threat.

Unlike the situation in huge conurbations such as London, Glasgow, Liverpool, Manchester and Birmingham, the tramway in Blackpool was never a rival of the railway but rather complemented it. Well almost. In the summer of 1898 the Blackpool & Fleetwood Tramroad was opened. The closest thing in Britain to an American interurban line, it provided an exhilarating high-speed ride along the coast through Bispham and Cleveleys to Fleetwood. From the start it carried vastly more passengers than the railway — indeed, it was the most profitable private tram company in the country, and its manager was paid the enormous annual salary of £700 plus a free house. It did not kill the Fleetwood railway but it certainly put it very much in the shade. Fleetwood eventually lost its railway in 1970 but the tramline is still there, long since taken over by Blackpool Corporation.

The Preston & Wyre Railway had a short independent existence. In 1849 it was absorbed jointly by the Lancashire & Yorkshire and the London & North Western companies. This could only encourage business from all over northern England and beyond, although Blackpool always tended to be rather resentful of this monopoly, particularly as the Lancashire & Yorkshire was the senior partner with two-thirds of the joint arrangements, and was not a company renowned for the quality of its passenger services.

Human nature and civic pride being what it is, it was perhaps only to be expected that just about every resort in the country came to harbour pretentions to middle class gentility. The trouble was that the citizens most desirous of such a state were almost always those in charge of businesses which depended on the hard-earned shillings and pence of the despised working class. Blackpool was no exception. As the attractions multiplied — the Winter Gardens, the piers, the Pleasure Beach, the electric trams — so did the thousands of working class lads and lasses, conveyed in very little comfort by the Lan-

cashire & Yorkshire Railway. In 1885 the Blackpool Herald remarked, 'During the best months of the year the town is deluged by the lower classes, and it would be unreasonable to expect the higher grades of society to mix with them'.

By now one station was insufficient to cope with the traffic. An isolated line had been opened between Blackpool and Lytham in 1863, but it was not linked at either end to the rest of the system. It was bought by the L&YR in 1870, extensively rebuilt, and re-opened, connected to the other Blackpool line at Kirkham, in 1874. Its terminus was named Blackpool Central, which indeed it was, being in the heart of the town beside the promenade and beneath the shadow of the Tower, erected later in 1894.

Blackpool Corporation was not especially enamoured with the position of the new Central station. It occupied a prime site and the line, running so close to the sea, forced future commercial development into a long thin southward-struggling strip between it and the beach. Eventually, after the best part of 100 years and many millions of free-spending trippers and holidaymakers later, Blackpool managed to get rid of its Central station.

In the meantime the Lytham line had pretty quickly became the principal route into Blackpool, although neither it nor the original Talbot Road one was particularly direct. By the turn of the century 60,000 passengers, a greater number than the residents of Blackpool, were arriving on a Saturday and the same number were departing. Probably there would have been more if the railway could have carried them. Further expansion of the railway facilities was clearly necessary and on 21 April 1903 a new line $6\frac{3}{4}$ miles long from Kirkham to a junction with the Blackpool Central line at what is now the South station was opened. At the same time the tracks between Preston and Kirkham were quadrupled. The new line proved its worth immediately, being almost exclusively used by excursion trains. The two terminus stations at Blackpool boasted no fewer than 30 platform faces between them and Spen Dyke, one of the three signal boxes controlling movements in and out of the South station, was the largest on the L&YR.

The First World War saw Blackpool busier than ever. The 1914 illuminations went ahead and before the year was out the first of 14,000 troops who were to be billeted on the Blackpool landladies arrived. Wounded soldiers also came to Blackpool to convalesce, all brought by train. Many resorts in other parts of England were almost deserted, but trippers and holidaymakers continued to pour into Blackpool.

With the end of the war the railways had lost their monopoly and the charabanc provided increasing competition. But there was plenty of business for everyone. In 1919 413,000 passengers arrived in Blackpool by train on the eleven Saturdays of the summer season. Chaos ensued, and frightening scenes were enacted as the vast crowds struggled to board the trains. To bring order and ensure that everyone had seats, passengers were allocated reservations and without them they were not allowed to board; such regulated travel became a feature of Blackpool traffic for many years.

Despite the severe unemployment suffered by so many, the late 1930s saw Blackpool booming as almost never before. One Saturday in August 1935, 467 trains arrived and departed from the two stations.

Business travel had long been a feature of the Manchester to Blackpool line. With the opening of the new line the 08.04 from Blackpool South, with its specially-built club cars, got the city gents into Manchester Victoria at 09.11, stopping at Preston and Salford. The return working was non-stop, but slipped a carriage at Bolton. By 1935 the slip carriage had gone but the time was down to less than an hour. Fifty-eight minutes for $45\frac{1}{2}$ miles may not sound anything wonderful, but it was a difficult route to work and finding a path through the dense traffic encountered all the way from Manchester through Preston to the coast was no easy task. The six carriages of the principal business train of the early 1900s were magnificent vehicles with high, elliptical roofs, large picture windows and recessed, Pullman-style end doors, but these were very much the exception, for arc-roofed, four- and six-wheelers with their hard, scratchy horsehair seats were still commonplace and the early bogie carriages were scarcely less spartan.

Aspinall's unique, inside-cylinder 'Atlantics' were introduced in 1899 and they, with

A former L&Y 4–6–0 in charge of the Manchester to Blackpool Club train in about 1928. (*Author's collection*)

the Hughes four-cylinder 4–6–0s which came out in 1908, had charge of the principal Blackpool-Manchester workings until well into LMS days. Of course at holiday times just about anything which could raise steam was likely to find itself trundling towards Blackpool and 4–4–0s, 0–6–0s and 2–4–2Ts were familiar work-horses.

Hughes became the first CME of the LMS and his first design was a 4–6–4T, a tank engine version of his 4–6–0s. Imposing through these latter might have been — and they were nicknamed 'Dreadnoughts' — they did not live up to their appearance. The 4–6–0s fared better and were associated with the Manchester to Blackpool route for over 40 years. They first appeared on the Club trains when brand new in 1908, and 20 of them were still shedded at Blackpool in 1935, despite the advent of LMS-designed 'Patriot', 'Jubilee' and '5MT' 4–6–0s. One of these, 'Patriot' No 5524, was named *Blackpool* and put in charge of the new Euston to Blackpool 'Fylde Coast Express' which did the journey in 4 hours 22 minutes, 47 minutes faster than the best pre-1914 time. Nevertheless the London traffic, whilst it might attract a good deal of prestige, was incidental compared to the real bread-and-butter business with Manchester and the rest of Lancashire.

Although scrapping had begun in 1925, there were still 11 Hughes 4–6–0s at Blackpool in 1939, painted in the beautiful crimson livery reserved for the principal passenger engines and regularly seen in charge of the Club trains. Six lasted into British Railways days and the final one, No 50455, ended its days at Blackpool Central shed, hauling an enthusiasts excursion to York and back on 1 July 1951 before being broken up at Horwich in the autumn of that year.

The last peacetime summer for six years saw the railways carrying a record-breaking number of passengers to Blackpool, many of them no doubt sensing that they might never again be able to sample the unique talents of Gracie Fields, George Formby, Reginald Dixon, and all that the greatest centre of entertainment in the Kingdom had to offer.

Just as it had 25 years earlier, Blackpool in 1939 found itself busier, if anything, in wartime than in peace. Some 37,500 children were evacuated from the industrial towns in September of that year, civil servants and the military soon followed, the allocation of engines to the two Blackpool sheds, which had been cut back to 30, was restored to 52, and the holidaymakers continued to come in almost peacetime numbers. With petrol rationed, the trams carried enormous numbers of passengers. The town was lucky to largely escape the attentions of the Luftwaffe, and although a bit shabby and rundown was ready to welcome the greatest number of passengers ever to arrive by train on one day, 102,889 on Wakes Week Saturday, 28 July 1945.

Throughout the later 1940s and into the 1950s full employment ensured booming business for the railways and the tram and coach companies. The 1960s changed all that, dramatically, Britain's first section of motorway, around Preston, had already opened and the era of holidays by car had begun. Fewer and fewer holidaymakers and day-trippers arrived by train and on 2 November 1964 the town's long-avowed ambition to get rid of Central station was realized. The direct line, dating from 1903, also closed, and 24 acres of station, engine sheds, railwaymen's hostel and sidings were sold to the corporation for £950,000. The corporation publicly admitted it had got 'a bargain', although it was several years before it began to redevelop the site. In the meantime, the derelict railway land served, as in so many other places, as a car park.

The trams, too, were under threat. The first route closures came in 1961 and others followed, including that to North station in the autumn of 1963. This left only the principal promenade route from the Lytham St Annes boundary at Squires Gate to Fleetwood. That winter even this closed down, except for the Cleveleys to Fleetwood section, although it reopened next spring. No Central station, no trams — what had Blackpool come to?

Left A Manchester express pulling out of Blackpool North station in April 1985.

Below The new Blackpool Pleasure Beach station, April 1987.

Steam trains continued to operate from Blackpool almost to the end of BR steam in August 1968. One might have thought that the Lancashire & Yorkshire Railway, pioneers in electrification, would have considered electrifying its busy Blackpool route, but it didn't and although electric trains have been operating through Preston on the main line since the early 1970s, the Crewe-Glasgow scheme being inaugurated in May 1974, there seems little likelihood of the diesels which have had a monopoly of the Preston-Blackpool lines since 1968 being displaced. Blackpool North, which had once again become the principal station for the town, had its original buildings demolished in 1974. The replacement was a quite pleasing reinforced concrete structure providing a bright, spacious concourse, buffet, bookstall and all the usual offices. There are eight platforms, all controlled by a big Lancashire & Yorkshire-built signal box. In this respect modernization has not caught up, for I counted in April 1988 11 signal posts sporting 23 semaphores and not a colour light to be seen.

The decline of the line which once served Blackpool Central has been quite extraordinary. The great iron road bridges which spanned the many tracks and sidings associated with it now pass over either derelict land or dual carriageways, and one solitary

line suffices to serve the terminus at Blackpool South which consists of an unsignalled, unstaffed platform bereft of any buildings. A holidaymaker of any period up to the middle 1960s returning to the site would scarce believe such a complex of railway installations could all but vanish; he might also wonder how Blackpool could cater for the arrival and departure of its visitors without them, but seemingly it can. Yet holidaymakers, trippers, conference delegates and, not least, residents still come and go from Blackpool by train. The town seems to have countered the threat of the foreign holiday and is doing good business. Its trams have survived, celebrated their centenary and prospered, and with the opening of the modest but attractive new Pleasure Beach station between South and Squires Gate stations in 1987, we may hope that the railways of Britain's greatest resort will also prove equally resilient.

Southport

As the crow — or seagull — flies, Southport is only ten miles from Blackpool, across the expanse of mud flats of the Ribble estuary. It is a lot further by rail and road, for there is no crossing of the Ribble until Preston, but the proximity of the greatest resort of all has always had a profound effect upon Southport.

Southport has a distinctive character all its own but one always feels it is casting uneasy, part disapproving, part envious glances across the water. The rivalry between the two goes back to the early 1800s. Southport's first hotel was put up in the late 1790s and at that time it was known as Churchtown, an area to the north-east of the present-day town centre which used to have its own station on the Preston line. Southport grew very quickly and in 1851, three years after its first railway had opened, its population of 5,500 was almost double that of Blackpool, and as late as 1901 it was still slightly ahead, 48,000 against 47,000. A guide published in 1851 declared that Blackpool was 'more select than Southport', which must have come as a bit of a surprise to some.

The first train to reach Southport steamed in on 24 July 1848. It started from Waterloo, where the Mersey reaches the Irish Sea. It was meant to come from Liverpool, but the Liverpool, Crosby & Southport Railway

A former Lancashire & Yorkshire 2–4–2T at Southport Chapel Street in 1958. (*Colour-Rail*)

which owned it found itself short of funds, and although Waterloo is today a suburb of Liverpool, it was then quite remote from the city and an omnibus was provided to convey passengers the five miles out to the railhead. Eventually the connection was made between Waterloo and Bootle and through trains began running from Liverpool Exchange to Southport in October 1850.

This gave Southport a tremendous boost. Liverpool was only 20 miles away and the crowds came pouring out for a day by the sea whilst the merchants built themselves fine villas and travelled daily into their offices, many of which were within a minute or so's walk of Exchange station.

Next came the line from Manchester in April 1855. At Burscough bridge it crossed the Liverpool to Preston line and a junction was put in so that trains could run direct from Southport to Preston. By 1855 the Lancashire & Yorkshire had sole control of both routes into Southport and its terminus station at Chapel Street, and in that year erected an engine shed at Derby Road which is the predecessor of the one which still stands on the site today. Southport now really came into its own.

The Floral Hall, where high class entertainments were staged, was built, whilst Lord Street, a wide, tree-lined avenue with handsome wrought-ironwork framing glass arcades in front of elegant shops, was said to be the 'finest street in England' and certainly far outstripped anything Blackpool could boast. Manchester cotton magnates built Italianate villas next door to the Liverpool ship-owners and played golf with them at Royal Birkdale. A horse tramway opened between Birkdale station and the Botanic Gardens in 1873, and despite being 15 years behind Blackpool in introducing electrification, Southport could boast in the period immediately after the First World War that it had 'probably a greater length of tramway in proportion to population than any town in the kingdom'.

Southport had magnificent sands but there was one drawback to them. They sloped so gently that at low tide the sea disappeared almost from sight. Although a promenade was built it soon found itself at such a distance from the sea that ornamental gardens were installed in front of it. The pier was no less than 1,150 yards long with a railway running its entire length, but it was nevertheless completely out of the water at low tide. From 1905 to 1950 the line was electrically operated, since when diesels have provided the motive power.

In 1880 the Cheshire Lines Committee decided it was entitled to a slice of the lucrative Southport traffic and in August 1881 opened a line from Aintree to Birkdale which it extended into the heart of Southport to a terminus at Lord Street a year later, the line running literally through the sand dunes. The station at Birkdale was entitled Palace on account of the great gothic pile of the Palace Hotel erected alongside.

Although Southport had a reasonably direct route to Preston by way of the junction at Burscough Bridge, the shortest route was that alongside the Ribble estuary. There was little population hereabouts, chiefly market gardeners, and it was not until September 1882 that a railway line penetrated it when the West Lancashire Railway was completed between Southport and Preston. This had its own station in Southport, just down the road from Chapel Street, and it was used until April 1901, when Preston trains did the sensible thing and took themselves off to Chapel Street, leaving their original premises to become a goods depot. By this date the line had been absorbed by the L&YR, which had taken it over in July 1897.

This was not quite the final development in the expansion of the railway scene in Southport, for the West Lancashire was involved in a third line to Liverpool. This ran from Meols Cop, the third station on the Manchester line, to a junction with the Cheshire Lines Committee route from Lord Street at Altcar. It never carried much traffic; the L&Y introduced railmotors in 1904, and passenger services ended in September 1938.

The great city and port of Liverpool was served by an immense network of railways,

but by the beginning of the twentieth century the inner suburban lines, on both sides of the Mersey, were beginning to lose business to the newly electrified tramways, which were both numerous and widespread. The Lancashire & Yorkshire Railway was quick to respond and although its line to Southport was not the first electric railway in the city — this honour belonged to the Liverpool Overhead Railway which, when it opened in March 1893, was the first electric overhead railway in the world. The Southport line was electrified in March 1904, and an interesting feature was that the third rail was extended beyond Chapel Street out on the Preston line as far as Hesketh Park, Churchtown and Crossens, which meant that Southport had its own suburban survice. All along the route residential development increased dramatically and in 1909 the St Lukes/Meols Cop/ Hesketh Park triangle was electrified, which was in addition an operational advantage for the principal repair depot was at Meols Cop.

The busiest routes in and out of Southport were always the original Liverpool line along the coast and the Manchester one. Just about every type of L&Y passenger engine appeared on the latter, the 'Atlantics' and the 'Dreadnought' 4–6–0s featuring largely on the residential expresses with their corridor stock introduced in the early 1900s. A new six-road shed was erected in 1891, and by later LMS days the Lancashire & Yorkshire types were giving way to LMS designs, chiefly Midland Compounds, Stanier 2–6–2Ts, and, inevitably, Class '5MT' 4–6–0s. There were, however, still the L&Y 2–4–2Ts and these lasted into the 1950s, ending their days in BR livery.

The Preston line closed in September 1964. It was steam worked up to the end and the 16-mile journey took just under 40 minutes. Nevertheless it was a most enjoyable experience; there were not many routes where you could travel in a complete prenationalization steam train by that date, and most of the few still existing were to be found in Lancashire.

One of the original L&Y-built Liverpool to Southport EMUs. (*NRM*)

Lord Street station and the line to Aintree had closed some considerable time before this, in 1952, and became a bus terminus. Being a Cheshire Lines Committee route, a variety of LNER rolling-stock appeared on it, as well as LMS, but it was only at holiday times that it was busy for as a commuter line it could not compete with the ex-LYR coast route which deposited its customers in the commercial heart of Liverpool.

The Southport electrics remained very popular and did great business and regulars could hardly believe it when the line was threatened with closure in 1967. Petitions were enthusiastically signed, public meetings held, and the danger passed but it seemed sheer lunacy that anyone in authority could ever have envisaged wiping out a service so vital to the Merseyside community.

A steam service continued to operate over the line for over 60 years after electrification. These were the through London trains. In later years they consisted of a brake composite and a second which were detached from a

Above Ex-LMS non-corridor carriages forming a returning Wigan excursion leaving Southport in June 1965.

Left An LMS-built EMU leaving Liverpool Exchange for Southport in January 1976.

Euston to Liverpool Lime Street express at Edge Hill and worked by a 2–6–4T over the otherwise by then freight-only Tue Brook line — which was always interesting — to join the Southport line at Bootle Junction. With the advent of through electric services between Lime Street and Euston the Southport carriages were withdrawn, but a pretty good substitute was a DMU service from Lime Street to Southport. This was threatened with closure in 1971 but it survived until 1977 when the underground link with Lime Street was opened, since when the Tue Brook line has reverted to freight only, apart from the odd special.

The 1939-built LMS electrics served Southport for 40 years. By the late 1970s they were well past their best, although they were still modern-looking and were wearing BR blue and grey livery. Much better riding Class '507s' began to replace them in 1979 and the last of the old units ran in ordinary service in the autumn of 1980. One two-car set has been preserved, based appropriately at Steamport, Southport, a preservation centre which began in 1971. In 1973 a lease was signed with BR enabling it to take over the old engine shed at Derby Road, which had lain empty since the last steam locomotives departed it in 1966.

The intricate network of lines and stations with which Southport was once endowed, over-endowed perhaps, has been greatly reduced since the 1950s, and Chapel Street station has had its frontage submerged in a shopping complex. However, services to and from Manchester and Liverpool are excellent, even if the once glamorous businessmen's expresses are no more. And the new underground system in the heart of Liverpool, which brought about the end of Exchange station and into which the Southport electrics have worked since May 1977 provide connections which had been dreamed of for generations.

Southport retains its air of considerable prosperity, particularly if one approaches it from the Liverpool direction, past avenues of the most select villas, which elsewhere would have long ago been divided into flats but which in Southport are still family homes. If the railway, which enabled the rich Liverpool and Manchester merchants to live beside the sea and so a day's work in their city offices, is less vital to the life of the town than it was in past times, it still has its part to play.

New Brighton and the Wirral

We have seen how Southport owed much of its popularity to its proximity to Liverpool,

The Liverpool Overhead Railway, Pier Head station, August 1955. (*Colour-Rail*)

but there was a resort which was even closer. That meant less in fares, a very big consideration in the days when every halfpenny had to be accounted for. That resort was New Brighton. Set right at the very tip of the Mersey, where it empties into the Irish Sea, it was the creation of an Everton speculator of the 1830s, James Atherton, who intended it as a development of superior villas for Liverpool businessmen. Its name leaves no doubt as to what was hoped of it. The Brighton of the North, no less.

The railway was a long time in coming to New Brighton. Plans were published in 1865 but nothing happened for two decades and it was not until January 1888 that the Seacombe, Hoylake & Deeside Railway opened its line from Birkenhead Park to Wallasey, extending it to New Brighton three months later; New Brighton was already by then a flourishing resort, much patronized by Liverpudlians and others, who before the railway arrived travelled by water.

Ferries on the Mersey probably date from at least as far back as the foundation of Birkenhead Priory in 1150. Some time after this Woodside became a landing station. A ferry service began from the foundation of New Brighton in the 1830s and huge numbers travelled upon it. Operated by Wallasey Corporation to Seacombe Ferry, a staggering 32,000,000 passengers were carried to and fro across the Mersey by the Wallasey Ferries in 1919–20. Not even the opening of the first Mersey Tunnel in 1882 and the electrification of the lines passing through it in 1903 could seriously challenge the ferries. In July 1904, Bass Breweries' annual outing from Burton-on-Trent to Liverpool and New Brighton required no fewer than 17 trains which arrived at Liverpool Central at ten-minute intervals from 6.40 am to 9.40 am, and for the trippers, the voyage and the sea breezes were all part of the day out.

Because it was the local people rather than the visitors who patronized the trains, when the visitors dwindled after the Second World War, and the ferry closed down in September 1971, the trains to New Brighton remained busy, the smooth-running Class '508' units providing a quarter-hour headway for most of the day, Mondays to Saturdays.

By the end of the nineteenth century the ferries and the railway had helped put New Brighton at the very forefront of British resorts. The GWR and the LNWR, who jointly owned the Woodside terminus at Birkenhead, put in a bid for the Seacombe, Hoylake & Deeside Railway, but they did not get it. Instead it merged with the Birkenhead dock lines to become the Wirral Railway. Woodside was the terminus of the Great Western's main line from Paddington, Birmingham, Shrewsbury and Chester. It would have been interesting to see GWR operation to New Brighton, but perhaps then the line would never have been electrified.

A third big company which had designs on the western bank of the Mersey was the Manchester, Sheffield & Lincolnshire, later to become the Great Central. This came up from Wrexham and connected with the Wirral Railway at Bidston. From there it ran to Seacombe, and when this branch closed in January 1960, New Brighton became the terminus. The future of the passenger service on that route has been threatened on many occasions but it has survived, although today it terminates at Bidston, where trains connect with the Wirral electrics.

The Wirral Railway got permission to proceed with electrification in 1900 at the same time as the Mersey Railway, but unlike the latter it did not take up these powers. Its steam trains continued to connect with the electrics at Birkenhead until the Grouping and afterwards, as part of the LMS. The latter, taking advantage of financial help from the Government to relieve unemployment, which was particularly severe on Merseyside, introduced electric working in 1938.

The Mersey Railway cannot really be said to have been a seaside railway for its chief purpose was to provide a link between the teeming banks of the river from which it took its name and to carry under it those whose occupations took them from Cheshire to Lancashire and vice versa. Nevertheless it plays

its part in our story for it was eventually to become an integral part of a system which would include both the New Brighton and West Kirby lines. Opened by the Prince of Wales in January 1886, it did great business for a while but found the competition of the ferries hard to come to terms with and only managed it when the line was electrified in May 1903. The carriages of the electric multiple units were highly distinctive being of purely American design, despite being mostly built in Shropshire!

When the former Wirral lines of the LMS were electrified, common sense prevailed and the two systems were partly integrated so that trains worked right through from both West Kirby and New Brighton under the Mersey to Liverpool. The West Kirby line dated from 1878, although the section from Birkenhead to Hoylake was six years older, having opened in July 1866. There are extensive sandy beaches running the length of the north Wirral coast from New Brighton to West Kirby, but although Hoylake had once been a port for Ireland it took some while to develop as the residential resort it would eventually become, and it was not until the Wirral improved the line in the late 1890s that it came into its own.

At West Kirby the Wirral Railway connected with a branch of the Birkenhead Joint line, the same railway which ran into Birkenhead Woodside and connected with the Mersey Railway at Rock Ferry. This, it will be recalled, was the joint property of those giants, the GWR and the LNWR. The LMS actually detached a carriage from a Euston to North Wales express and ran it over this line via the junction at West Kirby and on to New Brighton.

Like the Hooton to West Kirby line and the Liverpool Overhead Railway, the Mersey Railway-built electrics met their end later in 1956, and the trains which replaced them were virtually identical to the LMS-built units of 1938. These closely resembled the Southport and Ormskirk ones of a year later, although somewhat smaller in section in order to negotiate the tunnel sections. Many of the

stations were rebuilt in reinforced concrete, which gives them a distinct period flavour, whilst the terminus at West Kirby has recently and most successfully been restored and modernized, the façade facing the beach and the Dee estuary a couple of minutes walk away incorporating a parade of shops.

From 1956 the working of the former Mersey and Wirral Railway routes was totally integrated. It was taken a most significant step forward with the opening of the loop under the heart of Liverpool in May 1977 which enabled trains to continue beyond James Street, through Moorfields, which replaced Exchange, on to Lime Street, round through Central, now only an underground station, back to St James and home again under the Mersey.

The opening of road tunnels had long sent the ferries into retreat. The New Brighton ferry ceased in the early 1970s and with rail traffic on the Mersey network increasing by 27 per cent after the opening of the loop line, the remaining Woodside and Wallasey to Liverpool Pierhead routes were further threatened, although at the time of writing they still continue. It would be a tragedy if they disappeared for they provide quite the finest way of observing the handsome Liverpool waterfront and the still varied shipping scene, even if this, like the ferries, is a pale shadow of what it once was.

New Brighton has changed too. The trippers and holidaymakers have largely deserted it for more exotic delights and whilst its funfair and impressive 1930s open-air swimming pool remain, today it is a rather quiet seaside town. If anything its character is closer to that of Hove than Brighton, and far removed from the media-image of depressed, poverty-stricken Merseyside. The beach and the views are as fine as ever, the original red brick station buildings beside Victoria Road remain (although the reinforced concrete platform awnings are more recent), whilst LMS-designed semaphore signals are a feature of the line between Birkenhead Park and New Brighton, and indeed that to West Kirby as well. The Class '508' emus which work the

A Class '508' EMU approaching New Brighton from Liverpool in June 1988.

Wirral routes are most comfortable — and totally lacking in graffiti — a great improvement on the LMS-designed units they re-placed in the early 1980s. The journey time to the centre of Liverpool is a mere 20 minutes and thus the trains beat all road competition and reap the reward with consistently high levels of patronage.

WALES AND THE BRISTOL CHANNEL

The North Wales coast

The first railway to serve the North Wales coast had little enough to do with the seaside as such, simply because it came into existence before the notion of the seaside had taken hold to any significant extent. Those who lived on the coast were engaged either in fishing or in the coastal trade, and the few visitors came neither to bathe nor to frolic upon the beach to but to gaze in awe at and climb amongst the majestic landscape of Snowdonia, lured by the writings of John Ruskin, George Borrow and others.

The railway was built principally for strategic purposes, to speed up communications between London and the Irish capital, Dublin, and to get English officials and military personnel there as quickly as possible. Not that the sea didn't rapidly make its presence felt, for it occasionally breached the workings before the line was complete.

The Chester & Holyhead was an independent company formed to link up with the Chester & Crewe Railway which had opened in August 1842, and its engineer was Robert Stephenson. The Chester & Crewe connected with the Grand Junction, which had got to Birmingham in July 1837. The London & Birmingham reached the Midland city in September 1838 and thus by the end of the summer of 1842 a through route was open from Euston to Chester. Bangor was reached in May 1848, and although the line across the Isle of Anglesey to Holyhead was opened a few months later, passengers had to dismount at Bangor and travel across the Straits by coach over Telford's suspension bridge until Robert Stephenson's equally famous Britannia tubular bridge was ready. The first train rumbled across it on 18 March 1850, by which time the four companies which owned the various bits of the London to Holyhead

A LNWR 'Experiment' 4–6–0 with an up express at Colwyn Bay *circa* 1910. (*Author's collection*)

route had amalgamated to form the London & North Western Railway.

The coming of the railway transformed the coast of North Wales. It was now within five hours of London, two hours of Manchester and one and a half of Liverpool. For much of the 85 miles between Chester and Holyhead the railway ran within sight of the sandy beaches, and all along it, amongst the isolated clusters of fishermen's cottages, boarding houses, hotels and various amenities for the holidaymaker began to appear. The once flourishing coastal traffic, which had carried much of the slate from the quarries of Snowdonia, died almost totally although pleasure steamers became popular and linked a number of resorts with the Isle of Man.

The original stations of Queens Ferry, Flint, Holywell, Mostyn, Prestatyn, Rhyl, Abergele, Conway, Aber and Bangor were added to, the most significant being Colwyn, within a year of the line's opening, and Llandudno, which was served by its own branch from October 1858.

Llandudno, which was to become pre-eminent amongst North Wales resorts, virtually owes its existence to the railway. The

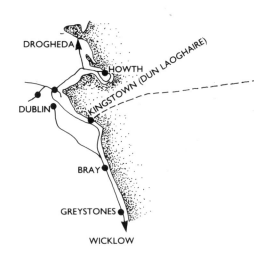

most spectacular watering place along the coast, set around a bay between the Little and Great Orme headlands, its population barely exceeded 1,000 in 1850, although this was a dramatic enough increase over the handful of fishermen who had been the sole occupants until the railway arrived at what is now Llandudno Junction, one of the most important stations along the coast and some three miles away across the estuary from Conway, which, with its celebrated castle through the walls of which Stephenson drove his railway —

The Great Orme cable tramway, August 1989.

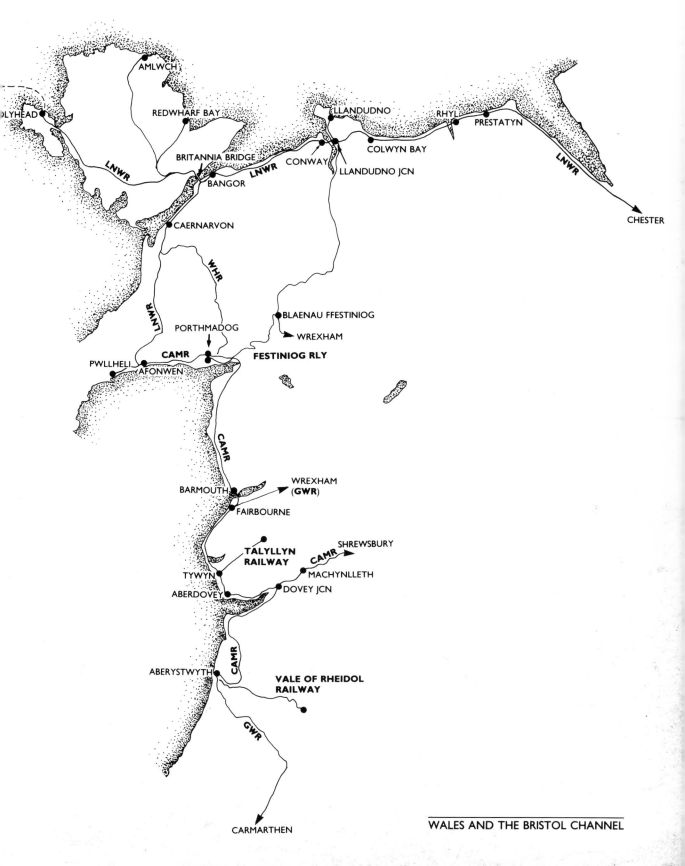

AMLWCH

REDWHARF BAY

HOLYHEAD

LLANDUDNO

RHYL

PRESTATYN

COLWYN BAY

BRITANNIA BRIDGE

LNWR

CONWAY

LNWR

BANGOR

LLANDUDNO JCN

CHESTER

CAERNARVON

WHR

LNWR

BLAENAU FFESTINIOG

PORTHMADOG

WREXHAM

CAMR

PWLLHELI

AFONWEN

FESTINIOG RLY

BARMOUTH

WREXHAM
(**GWR**)

FAIRBOURNE

CAMR

SHREWSBURY

**TALYLLYN
RAILWAY**

CAMR

TYWYN

MACHYNLLETH

ABERDOVEY

DOVEY JCN

CAMR

ABERYSTWYTH

**VALE OF RHEIDOL
RAILWAY**

GWR

CARMARTHEN

WALES AND THE BRISTOL CHANNEL

astonishing — was infinitely older and more important. But once the delights of Llandudno had been discovered by the LNWR and its customers, it grew vastly whilst Conway stagnated. By 1885 the population of Llandudno had risen to over 5,000 and the station had twice been enlarged. It was close enough to Manchester for a regular businessmen's train, such as those from Morecambe, Blackpool and Southport, to be put in the 1880s with special club cars introduced in 1908.

In his novel *The Card*, Arnold Bennett writes of 'The North Staffordshire Railway's philanthropic scheme of issuing four shilling return tickets to the seaside', and Ruth, the heroine of the novel, chooses to visit Llandudno, that resort 'being more stylish than either Rhyl or Blackpool, and not dearer . . .' Llandudno did not merely have class; it also had a tramway which was opened in 1903 and carried holidaymakers up the steep ascent to the Great Orme; it was, indeed, the only practical means of getting to the summit for all but the most agile. Operated by cable, the tramway was an instant success, carrying 77,410 passengers in its first year of opera-

Conversation piece at Llandudno, July 1989.

ERON

ABERYSTWYTH

LAMPETER

CRAVEN ARMS

CRAVEN ARMS

ELLI

GWR

NEATH

UMBLES

SWANSEA

MUMBLES
PIER

PORT TALBOT

PORTHCAWL

ABERTHAW

BARRY

BARRY
ISLAND

CARDIFF

PENARTH

NEWPORT

GLOUCESTER

SEVERN
TUNNEL JCN

SEVERN TUNNEL

BIRMINGHAM

SEVERN BEACH

MR

GWR

AVONMOUTH

PORTISHEAD

PADDINGTON

WC&PR

BRISTOL

CLEVEDON

GWR

GWR

BATH

WESTON-
SUPER-MARE

GWR

BURNHAM-ON-SEA

HIGHBRIDGE

FRACOMBE

LYNTON

MINEHEAD

S & DJR

GLASTONBURY

R

L&BR

BARNSTAPLE

BRIDGWATER

LSWR

GWR

PADDINGTON

TAUNTON

EXETER

EXETER

WILL
NC

WALES AND THE BRISTOL CHANNEL

No 45115 heads the 11.15 Bangor–Scarborough past Llanfairfechan, on 24 April 1984. (*Wyn Hobson*)

tion, and still running today with its four original bogie cars. By 1901 the population of Llandudno was almost 10,000, but although still popular, this most elegant of resorts has grown relatively little since then; today its population is just over 13,000.

Colwyn, when the railway arrived, consisted of a manor house, three farms and some cottages. The effect of the railway upon it was possibly even more dramatic then on Llandudno. The sands proved an instant attraction, donkeys and a pier arrived, in 1876 the resort was renamed Colwyn Bay, and by 1901 its population was over 8,500. Old Colwyn had its own station, and Rhos on Sea, along the bay towards Llandudno, was swallowed up. Fun-fairs, a theatre, a zoo, golf course, bowling greens, tennis courts, a miniature railway, a promenade and all that the Victorians and Edwardians expected of a resort were provided, and in addition there were mountain walks up to the Colwyn Heights and beyond. It also became a shopping centre and unlike other resorts along the coast the twentieth century brought little decline in its progress and today, with a population of over 27,000, it is the largest town west of Merseyside.

The third of the three largest North Wales

resorts, and the nearest to England, is Rhyl. Endowed, like all the others, with fine sands, these have in the present century attracted vast numbers of caravans as has the somewhat smaller Prestatyn, its neighbour to the east. Indeed, the chief image of the North Wales coast today is of almost endless ranks of caravans set between the railway and the beach. It is not beautiful, but it is little use the railway complaining for the LNWR made a fortune in opening up the North Wales coast and if today most holidaymakers come by car or coach, their great-grandparents would never have discovered the delights of the golden sands if the railway had not introduced the two parties. A particular attraction for railway enthusiasts at Rhyl today is its miniature railway. It has a long history, being built by those famous model engineers W.J. Bassett-Lowke and Henry Greenly in 1911. It ran, and still does, for about a mile around the Marine Lake.

The Welshness, if one can write of such, of the North Wales coast has much diminished over the last 150 years. The English not only poured in on day trips and week-long holidays, but many of them also set up businesses to attract their fellow countrymen or retired here, and today one is hard put to catch a word of the Welsh language anywhere between Prestatyn and Llandudno. Mind you, just as on the Costa del Sol, move a few

miles inland, and one soon becomes aware that one is not in England.

The period immediately before the First World War was the heyday of the North Wales resorts, at least as far as the railway was concerned, and in order to cope with the vast demands put upon it the LNWR quadrupled its main line along the coast. Holidaymakers arrived by the trainload from Merseyside, Lancashire, the Potteries and the Midlands and every class of engine from the imposing four-cylinder 'Claughtons' to the ubiquitous 'Cauliflower' 0–6–0s, as well as visitors from other companies, would be called upon to handle the traffic. Even as late as the mid-1960s, Chester on a summer Saturday was a hive of activity with both steam and diesel-hauled extras queueing up to change engines and find a path westwards amongst the Shrewsbury and Paddington-bound Western Region trains, and head out over the Dee bridge to the coast.

The 'Royal Scot' 4–6–0s had a long association with the 'Irish Mail', although LNWR express engines could still be found on the North Wales coast at the end of the Second World War, and 'Britannias' provided regular 'Pacific' haulage in the 1950s and '60s; Stanier 4–6–2s were rare visitors. Today steam can still be found on the North Wales coast with the revival of special workings from Crewe to Llandudno and Holyhead in 1989. The original and imposing Class '40' diesel-electrics appeared in the late 1950s and worked much of the passenger and freightliner traffic between Holyhead, Chester and Crewe into the 1980s.

Although some extra holiday trains are still put on in summer, there is little need for quadruple track and nearly all of it was abolished in the late 1960s. A number of stations, including Llanfair PG, the one with the longest name in the British Isles, closed. However, when a youth accidentally set fire to the Britannia tubular bridge in 1970, all through traffic ceased, and Llanfair PG was re-opened so that a shuttle service could operate between there and Holyhead. A bus linked Llanfair with Bangor which became the temporary terminus of trains from Euston. The bridge was eventually rebuilt with provision for road traffic as well, and Llanfair PG, along with one or two other stations on the coast line, was permanently re-opened.

'Bulleid' 'Pacific' No 34027 *Taw Valley* at Llandudno with the 'North Wales Coast Express', August 1989.

Above No 6000 *King George V* at Chester on 15 November 1980.

Below No 34027 *Taw Valley* departing from Chester for Crewe with the 'North Wales Coast Express', August 1989.

'Sprinters' handle much of the seaside traffic, the principal passenger workings, as when the line was opened 140 years ago, being the Euston to Holyhead boat trains. These are made up of air-conditioned stock in the charge of Class '47s' between Crewe and Holyhead, electric traction taking over south of Crewe. Perhaps one day the overhead wires will extend along the coast to Anglesey.

Two branch lines in Anglesey which once carried passengers to the coast are those to Amlwch and Redwharf. The latter only lasted 21 years, from 1909 to 1930, but the former, although passenger services ended in 1964, still serves the chemical works of Associated Octel situated in the far north of the island overlooking the Irish Sea.

Holyhead to Dublin

The imposing red brick railway hotel at Holyhead, which so dominated the railway landscape, has been demolished and the station rebuilt although, unlike the unfortunate situation on the opposite side of the Irish Sea at Dun Laoghaire, it is still possible to alight from the train and walk straight on to the boat.

The Kingstown (Dun Laoghaire's original name) to Dublin line was the very first in Ireland, being opened in December 1834. Until 1980 the mail boat pier was served by a branch off the main line and through carriages ran direct to Heuston station, Dublin, and on to Cork and also, at one time, to Belfast and Galway. Unfortunately the tracks have been taken up, and although there have been various plans to reinstate the direct connection these have as yet come to nothing. Irish Rail claims that the substitute Heuston to Dun Laoghaire double deck bus service does the job satisfactorily, It doesn't, as anyone with a ha'pence of common sense and two heavy lumps of luggage would be able to tell them.

A DART electric passes one of the Martello Towers near Seapoint and Monkstown, August 1986.

Dun Laoghaire, or rather Kingstown, was a resort from early days, the grandest in all Ireland. The south side of Dublin was always the classiest and Kingstown, easily accessible by train, and later by tram too, but decently distant from the city, attracted the middle classes and the affluent Anglo-Irish. Band-stands, floral displays, high-spired Protestant churches, imposing villas and dignified avenues of family houses spread north and south along the sea and up towards the mountains.

At the end of the 1950s, the lines north and south of Dublin were still worked in-dependently, using a mixture of railcars and steam trains, those on the north side all still in GNR(I) livery, although the company had been absorbed by CIE a year earlier. Over the years through working between Bray and Howth, beyond Dublin, became the norm, latterly by railcars converted to push-pull units. By the early 1980s these were in a dreadful state, uncomfortable, worn out and fit only for the scrapheap.

Ever since Edwardian times there have been proposals for electrifying Dublin's subur-ban railways. In 1979 these at last acquired substance when the Government gave CIE approval to buy 40 two-car trains from Link-Hofmann-Busch which would operate on overhead line equipment supplied by Siemens.

The Dublin Area Rapid Transit (DART) electrics began work in 1984. They were fast, clean, comfortable, reliable and frequent. Dubliners fell in love with them. Travelling habits were transformed, property values along the already popular coastal communities south of the city increased rapidly, and, as I write, five years after the DART's introduc-tion, the dark and light green trains are if anything more popular than ever. The year before the DARTs were introduced, 5.4 million passenger journeys were made on the suburban railways of Dublin. Four years later this had risen to 15.3 million. No one ever smokes or puts his foot on a seat in a DART — not unless he wants a swift reprimand from a fellow passenger — and rubbish and graffiti are virtually unknown.

I will stick my neck out and declare that the finest bit of seaside railway in the British Isles is the $14\frac{1}{2}$ miles around the shores of Dublin Bay from Merrion Strand to Greystones. Trains emerge from under the stands of Lansdowne Road stadium, home of

Left Stormy weather at Seapoint station, Dublin Bay, 28 December 1981.

Above right Day-trippers arriving at Bray in August 1969.

Irish international rugby, and after passing amongst suburban terraces run beside the bay, a vast expanse of shallow, rippling water or, if low tide, sand. The Hill of Howth and the barber's-pole chimneys of the Pigeon House power station guarding the entrance to Dublin docks dominate the view to the east, ahead is the long breakwater of Dun Laoghaire harbour, whilst to the west are the Dublin mountains. The DART electrics stop at a series of stations so close to the water that in summer bathers sun themselves on the wall separating the railway from the beach, whilst in winter I've known occasions when passengers emerging from a train have received a faceful of the Irish Sea as it breaks across the platform.

With electrification a number of closed stations were re-opened and do such business that the wonder is how south Dublin ever did without them. Salthill, one of the re-opened stations, is virtually within Dun Laoghaire harbour.

West Wales

Back on the mainland, north-west Wales is another especially fascinating part of the British Isles for the railway enthusiast, for it is here that a rich variety of narrow gauge lines is to be found running down from the mountains to the sea. Their history, and those of other narrow and standard gauge lines which have disappeared, is far too involved for us to go into here in any detail. Suffice it to say that virtually all of them came into this world to serve the needs of the mining industry, usually slate, and those that remain do so on account of the tourist industry and the hard work of several generations of dedicated enthusiasts.

In March 1852 a line was opened from Bangor along the shores of the Menai Straits to the ancient town of Caernarvon with its magnificent Norman castle. Although independently owned, the line was worked from the outset by the LNWR, whose trains even-

tually reached the southern side of the Lleyn peninsula south-west of Caernarvon in the 1870s by way of the branch from Caernarvon through Pant to Afonwen and on to Pwllheli, although the Cambrian Railways had originally worked the southern section when it opened in September 1867.

Afonwen was the last but one station on the Cambrian main line which wound its way northwards around the shores of Cardigan Bay. The section from Dovey Junction to Barmouth opened in August 1867 and two months later the complete line to Afonwen and Pwllheli began to operate. Pwllheli, although not at the end of the Lleyn peninsula, was the last place of any consequence and therefore the obvious terminus. It possessed a natural harbour and eventually acquired a holiday camp, which was helped to keep the railway in existence. A commendable piece of enterprise during the 1951 Festival of Britain was the running of the North Wales Land Cruise train along former LMS and GWR lines; amongst the interesting carriages which graced the train was a former LNWR twelve-wheeler and a club car designed for, but never used in, the 'Coronation Scot'.

Although the former LNWR line to Pwllheli closed in 1964 it carried heavy holiday traffic almost until the end. A member of the Foxcote Manor Society and a former Chester engineman recorded his memories of a summer Saturday Manchester-Pwllheli train: '. . . usually hauled by a Stanier ''Mogul'' and worked forward by Chester men . . . often loaded to 14 coaches. I can well remember trying to wangle myself on to the job one Saturday when my sister and some friends were going to Butlin's by train. I had a chat with the guard and he let the girls ride in the van with him. It was the only vacant standing room on the train. Imagine it, 14 coaches crammed with bodies.'

The description of the picturesque Cambrian Railways route along the sea as a main line should not lead the reader into supposing that mighty expresses thundered along it at regular intervals. Quite the opposite. It was single track and the trains, what few there were, nearly all stopped at the many stations. It was a difficult line to build, particularly the section from Dovey Junction, where it connected with the Aberystwyth line, to Barmouth. This involved negotiating the marshes of the Dovey Estuary, passing through four tunnels, climbing the cliffs to Friog summit where an avalanche shelter was provided and finishing with the spectacular crossing of the Mawddach estuary. This latter waterway, although not deep, is subject to fast currents, and the viaduct which spans it has needed much attention over the years. A drawbridge was originally provided over the navigable section at the Barmouth end, and this was replaced by a swing bridge in the early years of the present century. For a while in the 1970s weight restrictions precluded all but diesel multiple units at a time when the very

future of the entire line was in doubt, but a more enlightened attitude saw the viaduct's restoration in the spring of 1981, since when not only diesel but steam locomotives have once again passed regularly over it.

For much of its journey, the train from Dovey Junction to Pwllheli travels almost within touching distance of both sea and mountains, and hardly anywhere in all the length and breadth of the British Isles are there finer views, those in the Barmouth area being particularly notable. At Porthmadog the line connects with no fewer than two narrow gauge lines, the Welsh Highland and the Festiniog. By travelling up the valley and into the mountains on the latter a connection can be made with the BR branch line at Blaenau Festiniog and thence down the other side of the Snowdon range to Llandudno Junction and the north coast. At Tywyn, between Barmouth and Aberdovey, the Cambrian connects with the Talyllyn, a 2 ft 3 in gauge line justly celebrated throughout the railway world as the very first railway in the British Isles to be preserved and operated by enthusiasts, and the setting of a number of the Rev W. Awdry's stories.

Barmouth itself is a most attractive little town. Like so many Welsh ports, the coming of the railway dealt a death blow to its commercial shipping industry — 318 vessels were built in or close to Barmouth between 1750 and 1865 — although a regular steamer service to Liverpool survived into the twentieth century. However, the town prospered in another way. The beginnings of a resort might be said to have appeared when the first inn for travellers opened in 1795 but the railway ensured that Barmouth became a fully-fledged watering place. By 1880 there were three hotels, four inns, two temperance hotels and 113 lodging houses. Barmouth has not grown greatly since then and it was not until 1933 that it acquired a promenade — opened by David Lloyd George, no less. It thus retains much of its Victorian character, and is one of the most pleasing seaside towns in the British Isles.

Until 1923 there was considerable rivalry

The Festiniog Railway, August 1982.

between the GWR and Cambrian Railway routes to Barmouth for the holiday traffic from the Midlands and the north of England. In the end the Cambrian won because the old GWR route was closed by British Railways. The Cambrian Railways' main line began at the small Shropshire town of Whitchurch, where it connected with the LNWR's Crewe to Shrewsbury route. In the 1950s, despite the fact that the Cambrian had been gone 30 years, the Western Region of British Railways still stuck to its routeing by that line rather than the much more logical one via Shrewsbury, whence most of the Cambrian section's through traffic originated. Of course when the Whitchurch to Welshpool line closed then BR had to make recourse to Shrewsbury.

The motive power when I first knew the line in the '50s was often Standard Class '4MT' 4-6-0s. These engines were ideally suited to the Cambrian and, with the 'Manor' 4-6-0s, powered the most important passenger turns until the end of steam. Nothing bigger ever ventured on to the Cambrian, no 'Granges' or 'Halls' and certainly no four-cylinder 4-6-0s.

Thirty years later, in the summer of 1987, I once again rode behind steam, on the 'Cardigan Coast Express' between Machynlleth and Barmouth. By good luck I chose one of the few really sunny days the coast had experienced, the sun breaking through as we curved away from Dovey Junction, that curious establishment built purely for the convenience of travellers changing trains and accessible to the outside world only by a footpath — or coracle, for there is no shortage of water hereabouts. Lower quadrant semaphores were to be seen in profusion, although they were to go within a year. We steamed along the shores of the Dovey, dodging in and out of the tunnels and graciously returned the waves of the few holidaymakers who were up and about. Our engine could not have been more appropriate, No 7819 *Hinton Manor* from the Severn Valley Railway, and long familiar with the Cambrian and West Wales, having been variously shedded in GWR and BR days at Whitchurch, Oswestry, Carmarthen, Machynlleth and Shrewsbury.

We alighted at Barmouth and immediately leaped into a crowded 'Sprinter' dmu heading back to the last but one station, Fairbourne. There we boarded the 15-inch gauge train of

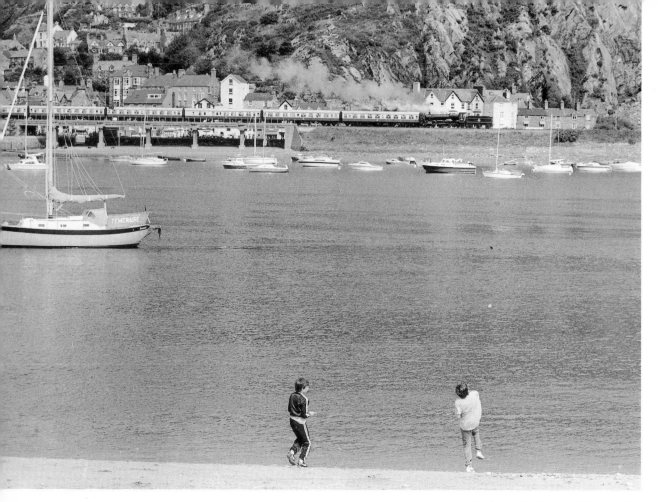

No 7819 *Hinton Manor* leaves Barmouth with the 'Cardigan Bay Express' on 17 August 1987.

the Fairbourne Railway and went puffing along the sand dunes for two miles until we found ourselves almost back in Barmouth but separated from the town by the River Mawddach. The Fairbourne used to be billed as one of the Great Little Trains of Wales, but of late the line has gone its own way and with much enterprise has increased both the locomotives and the number of passengers who travel behind them.

Aberystwyth, with its university and a history which goes back 6,000 years, is the most important place on the west coast of Wales. By the middle of the last century its population exceeded 5,000, and its fine sandy beaches were attracting an increasing number of visitors, despite their having to struggle over hills and mountains and along circuitous river valleys to reach them. Clearly it must have a railway, and in June 1864 the Cambrian Railways opened the line to Dovey

Junction, Machynlleth and the outside world.

Three years later, in August 1867, the Manchester & Milford arrived at Aberystwyth from Carmarthen and the south. Despite neither reaching Milford Haven nor getting within 100 miles of Manchester, the latter was a delightful stretch of railway. How could it be anything else when it served such unashamedly bucolic-sounding communities as Bronwydd Arms, Derry Ormond, Strata Florida and Caradog Falls Halt?

With the exception of a through train which ran all the way up the coast from Swansea to Pwllheli on summer Saturdays, traffic was generally very local and there was not much of it, nor ever had been, for the population in these parts has always been pretty sparse. There had only been three trains in each direction in 1902 and there were still only three in 1959. The line closed in 1965, although a short section remains, the $2\frac{1}{4}$ miles from Bronwydd Arms to Llwyfan Cerrig, which, as the Gwili Railway, became Wales's first standard gauge preserved line.

Above A Fairbourne Railway saddle tank waits for the off whilst across the estuary No 7819 *Hinton Manor* heads towards Machynlleth.

Below Replica Lynton & Barnstaple Southern Railway 2–6–2T No E759 *Yeo* on the Fairbourne Railway, 17 August 1987.

Despite their undoubted attractions, the scenery through which they passed and the fascinating and elderly motive power which worked many of their trains, neither of Aberystwyth's standard gauge lines ever achieved the fame which has lately come to the narrow gauge railway which runs from the resort for 11½ miles through the Vale of Rheidol to Devils Bridge. Opened in November 1902 it attracted both goods and passengers and did so well in the years up to the First World War that it prompted a successful take-over bid from the Cambrian Railways in 1913. When the Great Western Railway assumed a monopoly of the three lines radiating from Aberystwyth in 1923 — it had always owned the Carmarthen one — it built two new 2–6–2Ts for the Vale of Rheidol, based on the design of the original engines, and nine bogie carriages.

The line was closed during the Second World War but re-opened in 1945 and by the 1950s was being advertised by British Railways as its only narrow gauge railway; after 1968 it was also its only steam-worked line. Locomotives and carriages were painted in BR blue, which was considered by many to be drab and unimaginative, but nevertheless the three Vale of Rheidol locomotives could claim the unique distinction of being the only steam engines qualified to wear this livery

Vale of Rheidol 2–6–2T No 9 *Prince of Wales* about to set off from Aberystwyth in September 1969.

which otherwise was the exclusive preserve of diesels and electrics. However, the corporate image was abandoned during the 1970s and in 1988 the Vale of Rheidol was sold out of BR ownership.

Fishguard Harbour in March 1989, with the 01.50 HST boat train for Paddington about to depart.

RAILWAYS TO THE COAST

A branch ran from Lampeter, on the Aberystwyth to Carmarthen line, to the small port and seaside town of Aberaeron. This closed in 1951. Another branch to the sea, from the Fishguard main line to Cardigan, closed in 1962.

The Fishguard line itself is of more than passing interest, for it came into existence during the period from the end of the nineteenth century to 1914 when the ambitions and confidence of the Great Western Railway were in full flood and it was expanding and modernizing on every front. Locked in competition with the LNWR for the Irish traffic, the GWR operated from New Milford, or Neyland, to Waterford. However, this was a good deal longer than the Holyhead to Kingstown route of its rival and so, at great expense, a harbour was blasted out of the rock face at Fishguard. Together with the Great Southern & Western Railway in Ireland, a connecting line 37 miles long was built on the opposite side of the Irish Sea from Waterford to another new port, Rosslare, and amidst much blowing of its own trumpet the GWR began to operate boat trains to Fishguard in August 1906, whence passengers transferred for the three-hour crossing. The GWR had every right to feel pleased with itself for it now was joint operator of the shortest route between Wales and Southern Ireland. Although it could never seriously compete for the Dublin traffic, the Fishguard to Rosslare route has always been a popular and well-patronized one for travellers to Waterford, Cork, Kerry and the southern counties of Ireland.

Fishguard has a shingle beach at Goodwick, but its holiday traffic has never been really significant. However, elsewhere in this part of west Wales there are many very fine sandy beaches and the GWR built several lines which did much to popularize them and turn them into resorts.

Fishguard to Barry

The legend 'Paddington, Cardiff, Swansea and Neyland' borne aloft on the roofs of Great Western carriages caught my young imagination during one of my earliest visits to Paddington station. In those days, immediately after the Second World War when the bow-ended and 'Toplight' carriages were still painted chocolate and cream, the name Neyland had a ring to it which evoked visions

of I knew not what precisely but sounded splendidly romantic and mysterious.

The Neyland branch left the Fishguard line at Clarbeston Road, and at Johnston threw off another line to Milford Haven. Neyland lost its passenger service in 1964, but the Milford line survives and carries a good deal of traffic from the oil terminal there.

Tenby is an attractive town and the largest and most popular of the south-west Wales resorts. During the Napoleonic wars foreign travel became dangerous, so the fashionable few who could afford holidays looked around Britain and Tenby was one of the resorts which found favour with them. The railway arrived in 1863, a local line to Pembroke, but three years later it was extended north-eastwards through to Whitland and the main line to Carmarthen and beyond and the visitors then began to arrive in considerable numbers.

The station, built on a curve, is a short walk from the town centre and the cliffs and it is possible to stand on the station footbridge and look down the line towards the next station, Penally, and watch the HSTs running along the embankment which is all that keeps the sea from flooding the marshes behind. Lower quadrant semaphores and traditional GWR signal boxes still control trains on the branch, which vary from local DMUs to Paddington-bound HSTs and summertime holiday expresses to and from northern England. These latter terminate at Tenby but other trains run to and from Pembroke, ten miles further on, and the terminus at Pembroke Dock, another couple of miles.

Through Carmarthen and down the west side of the Afon Tywi estuary, the line rounds the headland to Pembrey and Burry Port. In the days when Burry Port was a thriving seaport it was served by its own railway, the Burry Port & Gwendraeth Valley, which was a largely mineral concern, and there were three stations in all on the coast. The BP&GVR was absorbed by the GWR in 1922, but a number of its 0-6-0Ts survived into BR days.

Llanelli is the next station and port eastwards on the main line. It too had its own mineral railway, the Llanelly & Mynydd Mawr; some of its 0-6-0Ts also lasted through 25 years of GWR ownership.

We have now entered the territory of industrial South Wales. Many and varied were the railway companies which ran up and down its blackened, teeming valleys, serving the almost countless collieries and the steel works and ports. Our concern, however, is with resorts, and we will leave the highly complex story of industrial Glamorgan for others to tell. Suffice to say that the GWR was the thread which held this story together and after 1922 it became the entire cloth, although it was cloth which from then on began to lose its lustre and sheen. This was not through any fault of the Great Western but because changing economic times after the First World War set South Wales on a path of decline which has continued down to the present day.

The vast band of workers which toiled to bring prosperity to the fortunate few in late Victorian and Edwardian times sent the coal they had mined down the valleys to Swansea, Port Talbot, Barry, Penarth, Cardiff and Newport, ports which as a consequence grew enormously. At weekends and at Bank Holidays the miners and their families travelled down the valleys to the seaside, and Mumbles, Porthcawl and Barry Island became resorts catering for day-trippers and holidaymakers in their thousands. The railway systems which served these resorts were unusually interesting, particularly those of the former and latter places.

Swansea is hardly the most prepossessing of cities, which is not to deny that there are those who have fond memories of it. In post-Grouping days it was joint GWR/LMS territory, and although the former was the dominating presence the latter nevertheless ran through carriages to and from London Euston by way of the picturesque and still surviving, but hardly direct, Central Wales line. HSTs provide a fine service out of the undistinguished former GWR station to and from Paddington today, and vestiges of the

many dockside yards and sidings survive. Much earlier than all this was the Swansea & Mumbles Railway which boasted the extraordinary title 'the world's first passenger railway'.

It began as a mineral line in 1807 and was the fifth public railway sanctioned by parliament. The other four did not — officially — carry passengers, but the Oystermouth Railway or Tramroad Company, to give it its proper title, did from 1807. Oystermouth is some six miles around the bay from Swansea, a long established settlement with a 12th century castle. The story of this ancient railway and its various owners and operators is highly involved, but suffice to say that it was horse-operated until 1877 when steam took over. Well, almost but not quite — for a short while Swansea street trams had running powers and worked their horse trams amongst the steam ones, which caused 'considerable difficulty', as was said at the time!

Just before the end of the century the line was extended for a mile and a pier and a hotel were built at Mumbles; other parts were

re-routed on reserved way along the sea shore 'which facilitated the traffic on the railway, in addition to effecting a great public improvement'. Mumbles became extremely popular. 'Amusements, entertainments and sea cruises' were available and in 1929 the line was electrified. Such a notion had been in the air for decades, ever since the electrification of Swansea street trams in 1900.

The Swansea & Mumbles trams were magnificent beasts. Dark red double-deckers built by Brush, they seated no fewer than 106 passengers which made them the largest street vehicles in the British Isles. In the summer of 1954 the railway became the only one in the world ever to reach 150 years as an independent undertaking, and great were the celebrations. In 1945 no fewer than 4,995,000 passengers had been carried, but by the mid-1950s competition from the buses of the South Wales Transport Company (who were the lessees of the tramway) and from private

A tram from Swansea at the Mumbles terminus on 20 May 1959.

cars had much reduced these impressive figures so that the 150th anniversary celebrations were also a valediction. In January 1960 this historic line closed, but the front end of one of the trams has survived and can be seen, along with various other mementoes and photographs of the line, in the fine new industrial museum in the revitalized dock area of Swansea.

The line from Pyle, on the Cardiff to Swansea main line, to Porthcawl, began as a coal tramway in 1828. Passenger trains did not begin for another four decades, and it was not until the present century that the extensive sands, the bracing air and the golf course really set up Porthcawl as a resort. In the words of the Rev. R.P. Griffiths writing in the *Great Western Echo* in 1985, 'It is hardly surprising to learn that the town was known as "The Brighton [yet another one] of Cardiff" on account of the crowds who came from the capital, and this is not to mention the swarms of people from the Welsh Valleys and beyond for whom it was the most accessible place for a day out or even a long holiday'. As the docks declined, so Porthcawl's fame as a resort increased and the *GWR Magazine* claimed that up to 10,000 would ar-

rive in one day by train. 2-4-2Ts and 2-6-2Ts were the usual motive power. Inevitably, perhaps, although Porthcawl continued to prosper in the post-Second World War years, its railway did not and the branch closed in 1963.

Further along the coast a branch, now freight only, still runs from Tondu, where the shed used to provide much of the motive power for the Porthcawl branch, through Aberthaw to Barry. This was built by the Barry Railway, a latecomer on the South Wales scene, but one of the biggest and most influential companies for all that. Other Barry Railway and Taff Vale Railway lines reached Barry from Cardiff. Barry docks exported vast amounts of coal up to the First World War and although a decline set in during the 1920s the docks are still in commercial use.

South-west of the docks the extensive sandy beach at Whitmore Bay began to attract visitors, a line was opened to Barry Island station close by, and so the most popular resort in South Wales came into existence. With its excellent rail links and its proximity

Barry scrapyard, May 1984.

to Cardiff, seven miles distant, the crowds poured in and the one-time fishing village was transformed. Rocky pools, bandstands, pony rides, horse and agriculture shows, and all that could be expected of a seaside resort were to be found at Barry Island. A large amusement park and a Butlin's holiday camp were opened after the Second World War and the 0–6–2Ts which were such a feature of the South Wales lines, on both goods and passenger work, found themselves as busy as ever.

Diesel railcars took over in the early 1960s and, unlike many other Welsh seaside branches, the Barry Island line continued to do good business. But, as all enthusiasts know, steam did not disappear altogether from the area for long lines of withdrawn locomotives assembled in Dai Woodham's yard between Barry and Barry Island stations. The majority were of Great Western origin and instead of being broken up, as happened in other South Wales yards, they lingered on; eventually almost all made their way out of the graveyard to various preservation centres and many are now once again hard at work — an extraordinary return from the dead. A number of 0–6–2Ts and 2–6–2Ts, once

familiar in the Welsh valleys, are amongst the survivors.

The Severn Estuary

From Cardiff the South Wales main line runs north-east to Newport, where steam trains still can be seen crossing the high bridge over the River Usk and where a number of freight-only branches serve the docks which extend to the estuary. Beyond Newport the line steadily closes on the sea, past the vast Llanwern steel works, until it reaches Severn Tunnel Junction, whose huge marshalling yards have recently closed. Immediately beyond them the old main line diverges north-eastwards to run along the banks of the Severn, which in places is well over a mile wide, to Gloucester, passing on its way Lydney where the preserved Dean Forest Railway, which possesses at least two GWR tank engines rescued from Barry scrapyard, heads up past Norchard to Parkend.

A DMU running alongside the Severn Estuary south of Severn Beach in August 1987.

Bristol and London-bound trains meanwhile descend into the celebrated Severn Tunnel. At 4 miles 628 yards, it is the longest in the British Isles and was completed in 1886. Above it on the English side of the Severn Estuary is Severn Beach. The station consists of a windswept, almost empty platform, the terminus of a suburban service from Bristol Temple Meads set beside a large expanse of mud. In short, it has to be said that it is the least prepossessing seaside resort I have ever come across. However, back in the 1930s, when choice and money was in vastly shorter supply and the line continued on past Severn Beach station and curved inland to join the Severn Tunnel main line at Patchway, it was deemed sufficiently attractive for the LMS to run seaside specials to it from Redditch, Birmingham, Great Malvern and Gloucester. One trusts that the excursionists got their money's worth; but one doubts it.

The line between Severn Beach and Temple Meads is full of interest for the railway enthusiast. It runs through industrial Avonmouth and past the docks, where there are a number of sidings, then along the north bank of the River Avon, before plunging into a

tunnel in the Avon Gorge to emerge in elegant Clifton and join the main line into Temple Meads at Stapleton Road. On the opposite bank of the Avon is the Portishead branch. Portishead is an ancient port and the line remains open for freight, although it is hardly ever used; it is also a small resort, as is Clevedon a little way along the coast. Clevedon is quiet, select and popular, and its branch line was in latter years worked by a '14XX' Class 0–4–2T and an auto-coach which ran up and down to the main line at Yatton.

Colonel Stephens owned a light railway which ran between Weston-super-Mare, Clevedon and Portishead, and amongst the usual fascinating collection of second-hand locomotives were two Stroudley 'Terriers'. One was bought from the LB&SCR in 1911, the other from the Southern Railway in 1937. The Weston, Clevedon & Portishead had been bankrupt since the days of Edward VII but had been kept going by the receiver. It carried a certain number of holidaymakers, but when the Second World War broke out these disappeared and the line closed down in 1940. The GWR, which had no physical con-

nection with the WC&PR, bought it, never ran a train on its tracks, and scrapped most of the rolling-stock. The 'Terriers', however, were overhauled, repainted in GWR livery and in the fullness of time became British Railways Nos 5 and 6. One was condemned in 1948 and the other in 1954, leaving their Southern brothers to survive into preservation.

The GWR branches to the two smaller Somerset resorts lasted until the 1960s. Passenger traffic on the Portishead branch ceased in 1964, although there was a revival when trains ran into the Bristol docks and down to Portishead during the 'GWR 150' celebrations in 1985, and the Clevedon branch closed completely in 1966.

Weston-super-Mare is one of Great Britain's principal resorts and to it the GWR carried vast numbers of trippers and holidaymakers from Bristol as well as other parts of the West Country and beyond. Curiously, the station, built of stone and situated on a sharp bend, only ever possessed two through platforms. There was a short bay at the Bristol end but it was the four long adjoining Locking Road terminal platforms which handled most of the holiday traffic. As late as the mid-1950s some 30,000 trippers would arrive on a Bank Holiday to look for the sea — and it needs some looking for when the tide goes at Weston-super-Mare. One has the feeling it wouldn't be too difficult to walk across to Cardiff without getting one's feet wet.

Over 30 excursion trains might be needed, too many for the sidings to cope with, and they would be stabled all over the place, in goods yards and on the various loops between Weston and Bristol. Just about every class of Great Western locomotive might appear, from 'Kings' and 'Castles' on the regular Paddington and West of England expresses to Class '5' 4-6-0s from the LMS, and pannier tanks.

By the 1960s road traffic was the railway's most serious competitor. The M5 brought the North and Midlands vastly nearer the West Country, and the GW/LNW joint line by way of the Severn Tunnel, Maindee East and North Junctions, Hereford and Shrewsbury, which had once carried holidaymakers from Lancashire to Weston and further west, ceased to be used as a through route. All such

Left A wet and windy Saturday afternoon in May 1985 at Severn Beach.

Right A Bristol & Exeter Railway broad gauge 4–4–0 saddle tank at the head of a train from Bristol at Portishead, *circa* 1878. (*Author's collection*)

WALES AND THE BRISTOL CHANNEL

traffic was now concentrated on the former Midland line through Gloucester, Cheltenham and over the Lickey, whilst the extensive excursion station at Locking Road, Weston-super-Mare, closed in 1964.

Weston-super-Mare is situated on a loop off the main line, leaving it at Worle Junction and rejoining it at Uphill Junction. From the latter the line continues over the Somerset Levels where the wind can sometimes blow sufficiently hard off the Severn Estuary to have a noticeable effect on locomotive performance with a heavy load, particularly in steam days.

Somerset and North Devon

At Highbridge the West of England main line used to cross the Somerset & Dorset Joint Railway's branch to Burnham-on-Sea, some two miles away. Taking the Somerset & Dorset railway to anywhere was a sure-fire way of finding the most roundabout route, and although there used to be a connection from the GWR station at Highbridge, Burn-

ham was not of sufficient size to sustain rail traffic for long after the Second World War. Passenger traffic ended in 1951, which meant that Highbridge became the station for Burnham, as it still is. The S&D line to Highbridge lasted much longer, until 1966, and goods traffic continued to Highbridge Wharf, which the railway had hoped would grow into a large port, and to Burnham into the 1960s. John Betjeman made a TV film about the Highbridge branch, travelling behind a GWR '2251' 0-6-0 in a two-coach non-corridor B set and in the guard's van of the Burnham goods train. When he arrived he described the sea air as 'like wine'. Although the poet laureate's eloquence was lost on the accountants, not quite everything vanished for one of the '2251' Class, No 3205, was preserved and today is still at work, on the erstwhile Minehead branch, now the West Somerset Railway.

The fate of the Minehead branch has been quite different from that of the line to Burnham. In any case the two had little in common, apart from being in Somerset, for the Minehead line extended for some 22½ miles and served not just the ancient port at its terminus but several other seaside locations as well as some large villages. Opened

throughout by the GWR in 1874, it began life as a broad gauge line but these were the days of its infancy and before it reached adolescence it realized the error of its ways and converted to standard gauge in 1882. Minehead grew into a resort and there was plenty of business to keep the branch busy, not just in the summer but in serving the local communities all the year round. Trains ran to and from Taunton, although in summer through expresses came from much further afield, especially after Billy Butlin opened a holiday camp right beside the station at Minehead.

The branch was closed by British Rail in 1971, but plans were already afoot to keep it open as a private undertaking and a limited service began in 1976. It had been hoped that trains could run right through from the BR station at Taunton to Minehead; the track remained in place, but this has not so far proved possible. For some years the West Somerset Railway struggled to attract sufficient passengers and several times it was faced with severe financial crises. Although it has some beautifully restored stations and the countryside through which it passes is delightful, the trains themselves were at first pretty uninspiring.

Left Weston-super-Mare Locking Road excursion station, 23 June 1958.

Right The signalman at Blue Anchor, West Somerset Railway, looks down the line for a sight of *Evening Star* on a misty autumn afternoon in October 1989.

BEWARE OF TRAINS

GWS 2–6–2T No 5572 at work on the West Somerset Railway, 13 August 1987. (*M.F. Yarwood*)

Now all that is in the past. More dynamic management from the mid-1980s and the entry into service of first a GWR '4575' Class 2–6–2T No 5572, a type long associated with the branch and borrowed from the Great Western Society at Didcot, then No 53808, one of the two Somerset & Dorset Railway 2–8–0s to be rescued from Barry scrapyard, followed by the move of No 3205 from the Severn Valley Railway, plus various other visiting locomotives, has made the line far more attractive from the enthusiasts point of view. Regular steam trains have also brought in the holidaymakers who still flock to Minehead and the surrounding coastal and inland areas, notably Exmoor National Park. So successful is the West Somerset today that

a share issue enabled the railway in March 1989, with the help of Somerset County Council, to take out a 99-year lease on the line and thus ensure its long-term future.

Lynton and Lynmouth, the latter 600 feet below the former on the north Devonshire coast, have been called, in the fanciful manner of the Victorians, the 'Switzerland of England', and a cliff railway connects the two. They never featured on the main line network, but for 37 years a narrow gauge (1 ft 11½ in) line linked Lynton with Barnstaple, which was served by both the Southern and Great Western railways. Opened in 1898, the Lynton & Barnstaple was taken over by the Southern in 1923 which invested quite heavily in it and ran it with such efficiency that it could lay claim to be the best-kept narrow gauge line in the country. Sadly, its round-about route and slow speeds left it unable to

fight off road competition and, amid much regret, it closed at the end of the summer season in 1935. A beautiful replica of one of its unique American-built Baldwin 2–4–2Ts is at work on the Fairbourne Railway, some of the carriages have survived, and moves are afoot to return narrow gauge steam train travel to at least part of the former Lynton & Barnstaple.

Barnstaple, on the River Taw, is the principal town of North Devon and both the GWR and the LSWR were anxious to serve it. In 1854 a line from Exeter by way of Crediton reached Barnstaple and was eventually absorbed by the LSWR. The GWR, in the form of the Bristol & Exeter Railway, got to Barnstaple from Taunton in 1873. Ilfracombe, 14 miles away on the coast, was reached in 1874. Having been a port for centuries, the arrival of the railway saw Ilfracombe develop into a resort, one which could boast a particularly magnificent coastline.

The distances from Waterloo and Paddington to Ilfracombe were almost equal, $226\frac{1}{2}$ and 225, although the latter came down to $203\frac{3}{4}$ when the cut-off route by way of Westbury was opened in 1906. Expresses were worked by both companies and competition was fierce in the holiday season. In the Edwardian era the overall time from London had come down to around five hours, which was where it was to remain. Ilfracombe was one of the termini of the Southern Railway's 'Atlantic Coast Express' and after the Second World War Pullmans appeared when the 'Devon Belle', with its celebrated observation car, was inaugurated to and from Waterloo in 1947. The observation car was turned on the turntable at Ilfracombe at the end of each journey. One of the cars is still at work in Devon, on the Dart Valley Railway; the other is in San Francisco, having gone there with Alan Pegler's *Flying Scotsman* train.

The GWR route to Barnstaple, for decades virtually monopolized by Churchward 'Moguls', closed in 1966. The Southern line as far as Barnstaple, now part of the Western Region, still carries passenger and some freight traffic but it no longer continues to the coast for the Ilfracombe branch closed in 1970. Bulleid 'Light Pacifics' worked much of the Southern traffic from 1945 onwards and one of the rebuilt 'West Country' Class with local associations, No 34027 *Taw Valley*, was restored to service, far away from Devon, on the Severn Valley Railway at the end of 1988. Barnstaple station, rather woebegone these days, is almost within sight of the sea. The trackbed beyond the station now forms part of the coastal path.

POSTSCRIPT

And thus we have reached the end of our journey. We finish where we began, in the West Country. 'Yes, and with a resort which no longer has a railway station, typical of this particular story', I can hear the more cynical retort. I would not deny that the days have gone for good when tens of thousands might arrive at one of the great resorts at the beginning of Wakes Week or on a Bank Holiday, when even the smallest, one-horse-and-whelk-stall outfit would find itself inundated by intrepid trippers released from a slow, uncomfortable, overcrowded rake of ancient non-corridor carriages. As we approached the end of the 1960s there were those who predicted that all railways, except perhaps for a few commuter lines and a couple of inter-city ones, would soon disappear. Yet despite more than ten years of a Government in the United Kingdom which has no great love for public transport and an Irish one suffering severe financial restraints, rail closures have become something belonging to the past.

We live on islands where we seem to have got very close to the absolute limit on the number of roads and the vehicles we can squeeze on to them. The railway remains the safest and most efficient means of land travel and, is also the kindest to the environment. Lines and stations have re-opened, and British Rail has actively encouraged the preservation movement so that seaside routes such as the Swanage branch, the Isle of Wight and the Festiniog railways have prospered, and park-and-ride schemes at Looe, St Ives and elsewhere in the West Country are being officially supported.

And whilst the motorist frets and fumes in and out of traffic jams all the way there and all the way back, the rail passenger can sit in smug comfort and sweep past them. We can still take the train to Blackpool and Brighton, Scarborough and Severn Beach, Wemyss Bay and Weymouth, and many other seaside towns, cities and villages. While cheap air travel abroad to guaranteed sunshine means that the seaside resorts of the British Isles face an uncertain future, the railway, the greatest factor in their popularization, may yet prove instrumental in their salvation.

Left Barnstaple station in July 1989. The line on to Ilfracombe, once busy with holiday traffic but closed in 1970, lies rusting in the foreground.

INDEX